Workbook

SECOND EDITION

Martin Milner

HEINLE
CENGAGE Learning™

Australia • Brazil • Japan • Korea • Mexico • Singapore • Spain • United Kingdom • United States

HEINLE
CENGAGE Learning™

Go for it! Workbook 4, Second Edition
Martin Milner

Publisher, Global ELT: Chris Wenger

Editorial Manager: Berta de Llano

Director of Marketing, ESL/ELT: Amy Mabley

Director of Product Development: Anita Raducanu

Development Editor: Margarita Matte

Production Manager: Sally Cogliano

Senior Print Buyer: Mary Beth Hennebury

International Marketing Manager: Ian Martin

Interior Design/Composition: Israel Muñoz
   Olmos; Miriam Gómez Alvarado

Illustrator: Jaime Rivera Contreras

Cover Designer: Linda Beaupre

Photo Credits: **51**: left: POPPERFOTO/Alamy;
   right: Comstock Images/Alamy

ISBN-13: 978-1-4130-0031-3

ISBN-10: 1-4130-0031-2

Heinle
20 Channel Center Street
Boston, MA 02210
USA

Cengage Learning is a leading provider of customized learning solutions with office locations around the globe, including Singapore, the United Kingdom, Australia, Mexico, Brazil, and Japan. Locate your local office at **www.cengage.com/global**

Cengage Learning products are represented in Canada by Nelson Education, Ltd.

Visit Heinle online at **elt.heinle.com**

Visit our corporate website at **www.cengage.com**

Printed in the United States of America
3 4 5 6 7 15 14 13 12 11

Table of Contents

Unit 1

1 Complete the sentences and then complete the crossword puzzle.

Bill: The Bulls aren't doing (3 across) _____ this season, are they?

Andy: No, they're doing (1 down) _____.

Bill: You didn't see the (6 down) _____ last week, did you? I missed it.

Andy: Yes, it was really (5 down) _____.

Bill: It's 7:15 p.m. already. The game's (2 down) _____ starting, isn't it?

Andy: Yeah. And the sky looks a little (4 across) _____.

Bill: I hope it isn't cancelled.

2 Rewrite the conversation with the correct punctuation.

1. **Tim:** youre julies friend arent you <u>You're Julie's friend, aren't you?</u>

2. **Ann:** yes I am were in the same class _____

3. **Tim:** julie didnt come to the party did she _____

4. **Ann:** no she didnt shes at home _____

5. **Tim:** its a great party though isnt it _____

6. **Ann:** yes it is really cool _____

3 Fill in the blanks with the phrases below. Then answer the questions. Use short answers.

is it	are they	didn't you	aren't you	isn't it	wasn't it

1. You're Bill's sister, <u>aren't you</u>?   Yes, <u>I am.</u>

2. These hamburgers aren't very good, _____?   No, _____

3. It's really warm today, _____?   Yes, _____

4. That was a great party, _____?   Yes, _____

5. This isn't a bad game, _____?   No, _____

6. You went to the concert, _____?   Yes, _____

4 Write questions and answers about the concert. Use the words in parentheses.

1. (crowded) Q: <u>It's crowded, isn't it.</u>

   A: <u>Yes, it is. The "New Kids" are really popular</u>

2. (line moving slowly) Q: _____

   A: _____

3. (very good reviews) Q: _____

   A: _____

4. (not nice day) Q: _____

   A: _____

5 Number the sentences to make a conversation.

___ Great! Why don't you join us at break?

___ Herman and I play soccer together. You don't happen to play soccer, do you?

___ Yes, I am.

___ I'd like to introduce you to my friend Herman.

___ Nice to meet you, Herman.

___ Yes, I do actually.

<u>1</u> You're Bill's brother, aren't you?

6 Match the situation and the small talk.

✔ = definitely   ✗ = never   ? = possible but unlikely

	soccer game	party	pop concert	school cafeteria
1. It isn't a very nice night, is it?	✔	?	?	✗
2. That's a new dress, isn't it?				
3. This really is a bad game, isn't it?				
4. I'd like you to meet my cousin, Vera.				
5. It's a nice day, isn't it?				
6. This line isn't going anywhere, is it?				

LESSON B I'd like you to meet my cousin Brad.

7 Unscramble the following sentences.

1. you to I introduce to new Jim my friend want   <u>I want to introduce you to my new friend Jim.</u>
2. Pistons go see next I want week to the _____
3. meet I'd sister to like your _____
4. you to I'd to like classmate introduce your new _____
5. you parents my I'd meet like to _____

8 Read the article then fill in the chart.

When you meet someone for the first time, it isn't always easy to start a conversation. Here are some ideas that you may want to try.

■ Talk about something you can both see. For example, you might say something nice about the other person's shoes or clothing. But you should never say anything too personal.

■ The weather is always a safe topic. It's not too personal and everybody feels comfortable talking about it. But don't talk too long about the weather or it may sound boring.

■ Talk about something you are both doing - waiting for a bus, studying for an exam, or buying something in a store. Use simple language.

Do	Don't
Say something nice about the person's clothing.	

9 Every year there are some new students at your school. Write some DOs and DONTs about making small talk to the new students.

Do	Don't
Use positive body language. Smile and look friendly.	Don't be too direct. For example, don't say, 'Hey, my name's Ken. Would you like to go to the movies with me?'

Go for it!
What is a Wind Farm?

Read the article.

The first windmills were invented over 1000 years ago. They were found in China and the Middle East and were used to pump water and to make flour. They began to be used in Europe and England about 900 years ago. They were especially important in Europe and the Netherlands where they were used to pump water from land that was below sea level. By the 1800s, there were about 9000 windmills in the Netherlands. Windmills were also important in the settlement of the western part of the United Sates. They were used to pump water to irrigate crops and provide water for farm animals.

Modern wind turbine generators make electricity by using the power of the wind. This way of making electricity is very clean. It doesn't use up any of the earth's natural resources and it is free. There is one problem, however. In order to make electricity, the wind speed must be 13 miles per hour (21 kilometers per hour). There are not too many places that have that kind of wind. One place that does is the San Gorgonio Mountain Pass in California's San Bernadino Mountains. A company has built a "wind farm" there with more than 4000 separate windmills. They make electricity for the whole Coachella Valley in southern California.

Match each word with a word that means the opposite.

1. clean
2. free
3. below
4. western
5. always
6. especially

a. above
b. eastern
c. dirty
d. never
e. expensive
f. not very

Read the answers then write the questions.

1. Q: <u>What can windmills be used for?</u>

    A: Windmills can be used to pump water, make flour, irrigate crops, provide water for animals and to make electricity.

2. Q: _____

    A: They are important because many parts of the Netherlands are below the level of the sea.

3. Q: _____

    A: The advantages of making electricity from wind are that it is clean, it doesn't use up the earth's natural resources and it is free.

4. Q: _____

    A: The problem is that you need a lot of wind.

5. Q: _____

    A: There are 4000 windmills.

Unit 2

LESSON A
Learning a new language is fun.

1 Put a check mark ✓ if the words go together and an ✗ if they don't.

	grammar points	vocabulary lists	study groups	practice tests	flashcards
memorize	✓	✓	✗	✗	✓
make					
do					
enjoy					
form					
learn					

2 Fill in the blanks using words from the box.

| artificial | embarrassing | exciting | tiresome | challenging | frightening |

1. I hate standing in front of the class. It's really _____. My face always goes red.
2. Copying exercises from the board is really _____. It's slow and boring and I don't like it.
3. I really enjoy doing grammar exercises. They are _____ and they make me think.
4. Role plays are good fun but they are not like real life. They are a bit _____.
5. I learn a lot of English from Chat rooms on the Internet. It's fun! It's much more _____ than using a textbook.
6. Tests are _____. They make me really nervous and I never get good grades.

Verbs that take gerunds (-ing)	Verbs that take infinitive (to …)	Verbs that can take both
find can't stand spend (time) believe stop enjoy get tired of have trouble	decide pretend encourage want expect help forget try need	like love hate

3 Write the questions and answers using the words in parentheses.

1. Q: (like / read / don't you) _____
   A: (yes / read / every day) _____
2. Q: (get tired / look up / new words / dictionary) _____
   A: (No / never use / dictionary) _____
3. Q: (what / you / do) _____
   A: (find / guess / words helps me / remember them) _____

6   **LEARNING TO LEARN**

4 Change the verb in parentheses to the correct form.

1. I enjoy (do) role plays. They help me (practice) the language in a situation.
   I enjoy doing role plays. They help me to practice the language in a situation.

2. I find (learn) vocabulary lists difficult. But I do enjoy (read) stories and articles.
   _____

3. I want (travel) when I go to college, so I spend a lot of time (study) English.
   _____

4. I can't stand (memorize) grammar rules. I just want (speak) the language.
   _____

5. My teacher encourages me (speak) a lot. I didn't use to enjoy (speak), but now I do.
   _____

6. I believe (meet) and (speak) to foreigners is the key to learning a language.
   _____

5 Number the sentences to make a conversation.

___ I don't like memorizing words either but I just read the words aloud before I go to sleep and in the morning I can still remember them.

___ No, you need to write down the new words and expressions that you hear.

_1_ You always do well in English. How do you do it?

___ Okay! I'm going to try that. Thanks.

___ Ugh! I hate memorizing lists of new words.

___ Well, I always try to listen to as much English on TV as possible.

___ You mean all I have to do is watch TV!

6 Write questions from the table and then answer them truthfully.

Do you	spend time	to chat	books?
	get tired of	reading	films in English?
	have trouble	watching	mistakes?
	like	making	on the Internet?
	try	to memorize	with friends?
		to study	word lists?

1. _Do you spend time reading books? Yes, I do. I try . . ._ _____

2. _____

3. _____

4. _____

5. _____

6. _____

LESSON B I find parallel parking really hard.

7 Match the challenges with the solutions.

Challenges	Solutions
1. I have trouble understanding instructions.	a. Form a study group after school.
2. I find reading difficult because I'm slower than the other students.	b. Be confident! Prepare well.
3. I don't like to work alone. I learn better with others.	c. Listen very carefully. Watch what the other students do.
4. I find performing in front of the class very embarrassing.	d. Write a word list every day. Study it at night and then test yourself in the morning.
5. I have problems remembering vocabulary.	e. Read at home. Don't try to understand every word. Try to get the main points.

8 Read the e-mail and then fill in the chart with the ideas for making learning English easier.

Message

Accept | Reply | Forward | Delete | Print | Move to

From: Bruce Williams   Attachments:
To:
Copy:
Subject: Studying

You're right Carlos. I don't find learning English easy either. My friend Mario believes working in a travel agency helps him, but I think I learn more at school.

When we have tests, I find using my notes to review helps a lot. The book is good, but I write the most important things in my notes. My sister Alice says she needs to study with friends. But she won't study with me. And my friend Claire spends a lot of time making vocabulary lists. She says she needs to write words down in order to remember them.

Do you have any other good ideas?

Bruce

Mario	Bruce	Alice	Claire
▪ working in a travel agency	▪	▪	▪

9 What other ideas do you have to make learning English easier?

1 I find ...

2 I believe ...

3 _____

4 _____

5 _____

Libraries in the United States

Read the article.

During the early years of the European settlement of America, there were no public libraries. There were a few private libraries, mostly in the state of Massachusetts. In 1731, Benjamin Franklin founded the first public library in America in Philadelphia, Pennsylvania. In the beginning, people had to pay to borrow books from this library.

After the American Revolution in 1776, the number of free public libraries began to grow. These libraries provided a large variety of books for people to borrow. These included books about literature, art and music. Free libraries also delivered courses of instruction in practical matters such as farming.

Today, even the smallest community will have its own public library where books can be borrowed without charge. These libraries are paid for by town, city or county governments. Public libraries now meet a wide variety of needs. In addition to books, they provide music cassettes, books on tape, CDs and videos. Programs for children, a particular feature of U.S. and Canadian libraries, provide storytelling times as well as toys and games for children to play with. Most libraries also have computers which give users access to the Internet.

Circle the correct answer.

1. The first public library in the United States was started in 1776.	True	False
2. Most early private libraries were in Pennsylvania.	True	False
3. People paid money to borrow books from early libraries.	True	False
4. In the 1700s, free libraries offered courses in farming.	True	False
5. Some libraries provide games as well as books.	True	False

Match the word with the correct meaning.

1. founded	a. useful
2. private	b. special
3. couldn't afford	c. for free
4. practical	d. started
5. particular	e. didn't have enough money for
6. without charge	f. not open to most people

Read the last paragraph again. Use it as a model to write about libraries in your country. Are they the same or different? In what way?

_____

_____

_____

_____

_____

Unit 3 LESSON A
You used to be short.

1 Write the words below in the correct column.

| blond hair | introverted | outgoing | short | studious | tall |
| funny | long hair | serious | shy | straight hair | young |

Appearance	Personality
blond hair	funny

2 Look at the pictures of Judy and her mother. Then complete the sentences using *used to, didn't use to* and *use to*.

1. Judy ___used to___ have long hair.
2. Did she _____ have curly hair?
3. No, she _____ have straight hair.
4. Judy's mother _____ be taller than Judy.
5. Did her mother _____ have straight hair?
6. No, she _____ have straight hair.

3 Write the questions or the answers. Answer truthfully.

1. Q: ___Did you use to have long hair?___
   A: Yes I did, but I decided to have it cut real short.
2. Q: Did you use to play with dolls when you were younger?
   A: _____
3. Q: _____
   A: Yes, I used to be very introverted.
4. Q: Did your parents use to go to discos when they were in their teens?
   A: _____
5. Q: Did you use to be annoying when you were younger?
   A: _____

4 Complete the sentences using *still* or *anymore*.

1. I used to be short but I'm not _____anymore_____.

2. When I was a little kid, I used to be very shy. In fact I'm _____ not very outgoing.

3. My father used to be great fun when I was a kid but he's not _____. He's super strict.

4. I _____ have to do household chores even though I'm almost 17 years old. It's not fair!

5. I used to be good friends with Ivan but now he's too serious. I don't like him _____.

6. I had to go to the gym with my mother when I was younger. She _____ goes, but I stopped a long time ago.

5 Number the sentences to make a conversation.

___ But you haven't changed much. You're still tall and pretty.

___ Gee, thanks, Ramon. It's nice of you to say that.

_1_ Hi! It's Jenny, isn't it?

___ Ramon! Wow! You've changed a lot. You used to be short and real quiet. Not anymore!

___ Ramon. Ramon Perez. Don't you remember me? We used to be in primary school together.

___ Yeah, that's right. Jenny Brown. But I'm sorry, I don't remember you.

> **had to**
> *had to:* used to show you were forced to do something in the past.
> For example:
>   My primary school started at 8:00, so I <u>had to</u> get up at 6:30. When I was younger, I <u>had to</u> do lots of chores.

> **used to**
> *used to:* indicates something that happened in the past, but is now different.
> For example:
>   I <u>used to</u> hate math. Now, I love it!
>   I <u>used to</u> have short hair. Now, it is much longer.

6 Fill in the blanks using *had to* or *used to.*

1. When I was younger, I _____had to_____ do household chores.
2. I _____ watch a lot of cartoons when I was a little kid.
3. I didn't like my last school because I _____ wear a school uniform.
4. My grandfather didn't go to school. He _____ teach himself to read and write.
5. I _____ to love going to the beach, now I hate it.
6. I _____ play soccer every day, now I just don't have the time.

LESSON B I still sleep with the light on.

7 Read the sentences and fill in the blanks. Then complete the crossword puzzle.

Across

1. My brother loves mountain climbing. I could never do it because I'm afraid of ___high places___ .

5. I sleep with the light on. I'm still afraid of the _____.

6. My mother is really afraid of _____, so we have to take trains or drive for hours and hours. It's really boring.

7. I have never been afraid of _____. They're great fun to play with and take for walks.

Down

2. I used to be afraid of being _____ but now I enjoy just sitting in my room alone reading.

3. I really hate those nature programs on the TV. If I just see a _____, I get really frightened.

4. I used to be _____ of spiders, but now I quite like them.

```
¹h i g h p l ²a c e ³s
                a       s
        4               
        6               
                        
                        
        7               
```

8 Read the article then answer the questions using short answers.

The Real Story of Carmen Castillo

Interviewer: Thanks for talking with "Movie Life". What was your life like before you became a movie star, Carmen?

Ms. Castillo: Well, I used to work in a restaurant and live with my parents. At the weekend, I used to go to the beach with my friends. My life was simple and uncomplicated.

Interviewer: How have things changed?

Ms. Castillo: Well, I think I used to be happier then. I used to like going food shopping or just taking a walk. People didn't know me then. But now everybody wants to talk with me. I can't go out of the house anymore. So, now I stay at home and watch TV a lot.

Interviewer: That's not much fun.

Ms. Castillo: No, it isn't. I never used to be afraid of crowded places, but now I am.

1. Did Carmen use to live with her parents? _____Yes, she did._____
2. Does she watch a lot of TV now? _____
3. Did she used to be afraid to go out? _____
4. Did she use to go to the beach? _____
5. Does she go to the beach now? _____
6. Did she use to be afraid of crowded places? _____

9 Answer the questions to make a story about yourself.

When I was younger . . .

What did you use to look like?   _____

What was your personality like?   _____

What did you have to do?   _____

However, I've changed a lot.

What do you look like now?   _____

What is your personality like?   _____

The Industrial Revolution

Read the article.

Until the early 1700s most things used to be made by hand in people's homes, but when the Industrial Revolution began, more and more things began to be made by machines in factories. The Industrial Revolution began in England in the 1700s and spread very quickly. By the early 1850s, it had reached France, Germany and the United States. Next it spread to Sweden and Japan, and by the 1950s it could be found in almost every country in the world.

The Industrial Revolution caused several major changes:

- Many people who used to work at home began to work outside the home. Before this time, most of the things people needed were made at home. With the invention of machines to make clothing, furniture, and other goods, a new system developed. More and more people began to work in factories outside the home.

- In the early years, poor people had to work long hours in factories. Sometimes children as young as 5 or 6 were forced to work from 13 to 16 hours a day. In the early 1800s, one third of the factory workers in the United States were between the ages of seven and twelve.

- For the first time, many women began to work outside the home. Some single women left farming areas to find factory jobs, along with a more exciting life in the city.

Scan the article and fill in the blanks.

1. The Industrial Revolution began in the 1700s in _____England_____ (where?).
2. Before the Industrial Revolution, most people worked _____ _____ (where?).
3. After the Industrial Revolution, many people worked _____ (where?).
4. During the Industrial Revolution, many poor _____ (who?) worked long hours.
5. During the Industrial Revolution, many _____ (who?) began to work outside the home for the first time.

Match each word with the correct meaning.

1. by hand   a. move to other places
2. outside   b. things people need
3. spread   c. change
4. goods   d. without using a machine
5. revolution   e. away from

Write the questions or the answers.

1. Q: _____
   A: Yes, people used to make their own clothing and furniture at home.
2. Q: _____
   A: Yes, children had to work long hours in factories.
3. Q: Do children still have to work long hours in factories?
   A: _____
4. Q: Would you prefer to work in a factory or on a farm? Why?
   A: _____

LESSON A
I should be allowed to have a job.

1 Write a check mark ✓ in the boxes that make sentences with which you agree. Write an ✗ if you disagree.

	. . .their children to have a part-time job.	. . . their children to have a tattoo.	. . . their children to choose their own clothes.	. . . their children to go out with friends every night.
Parents should allow	✓	✗	✓	✗
Parents should force				
Parents should encourage				
Parents should expect				

2 Match the statements and the opinions.

1. Parents should encourage 16 year olds to have part-time jobs.

2. The government should allow 14 year olds to drive.

3. Schools should permit students to bring laptops to class.

4. Schools should not give homework at weekends.

5. Parents should allow teenagers to choose their own clothes.

a. I agree. They are old enough to know what they want and they will look after them better.

b. I agree. It prepares them for work after they have finished their education.

c. I agree. Students need time to rest after working all week.

d. I disagree. It would be too dangerous.

e. I disagree. Not all kids have computers, so the kids with computers would have an advantage.

3 Write three sentences from the table that you agree with and three sentences that you disagree with.

Parents	should	allow	students	to have a part time job.
		force		to have a tattoo.
Teachers		encourage	their children	to choose their own clothes.
		help		to do household chores.
		expect		to get a piercing.
		convince		
		require		

Agree

1. _Parents should allow their children to have a part time job._
2. _____
3. _____

Disagree

1. _____
2. _____
3. _____

4 Change the sentences from active to passive. Then say if you agree or disagree and give your reason.

1. Parents should allow their children to have a part-time job.
   <u>Children should be allowed to have a part-time job.</u>
   <u>I agree. I need extra money.</u>

2. Parents should encourage their kids play a musical instrument.
   _____
   _____

3. The government should allow 16 year olds to drive.
   _____
   _____

4. Parents should force their children to do household chores.
   _____
   _____

5. Schools should require students to wear school uniforms.
   _____
   _____

5 Number the sentences to make a conversation.

___ Well, in that case, no classes.

___ Well it depends. If it is an important subject, like Math, I think they should.

___ Then I think the kids should be encouraged, not forced.

_1_ Do you think parents should force children to do classes after school?

___ And if it isn't an important subject, for example, art or music?

___ And what if the kid still didn't want to do it?

6 Write sentences from the table. Then say if you agree or disagree with them and give your reasons.

I We Teenagers	should be	allowed permitted forced encouraged helped motivated expected required	to play a musical instrument. to have a tattoo. to choose their own clothes. to do household chores. to get piercings. to drive at 16. to stay at school until they are 18.

1. <u>Teenagers should be encouraged to play a musical instrument.</u>
   <u>I agree. Music helps people to relax. I could form a band and become famous.</u>

2. _____
   _____

3. _____
   _____

4. _____
   _____

LESSON B Steve convinced me to go hang gliding.

7 Match the three columns. Then choose one situation and write a dialogue between you and your parents.

Situation	Reason why	Reason why not
1. You took a book from the school library without permission.	I. She needed it for a wedding.	a. You will not get 100% attendance now.
2. You gave your friend your best new dress.	II. It was the last day of the semester and we never do any work.	b. You have never worn it and she may get it dirty.
3. You dyed your hair green.	III. I'm going to be a monster in the school play.	c. It's stealing. What if someone else needs the book?
4. You drove your father's car without permission.	IV. I needed it for an assignment and the librarian wasn't there.	d. It's completely illegal and you don't have a license.
5. You cut classes.	V. I had to take the dog to the vet. It was an emergency.	e. But your grandmother is coming tomorrow and she will be really shocked.

Parent: _____
You: _____
Parent: _____
You: _____
Parent: _____
You: _____

8 Read the passage. Underline Anna's reasons for going and circle Mom's reasons for not going.

Anna is trying to convince her mother to let her go with her friends to do a dance class for some senior citizens. However, Anna has been "grounded" for a week—she is not allowed to leave the house—because she got poor grades in her last school report.

Anna: Mom, my friends are going to do a dance class for seniors. We need three people and if I can't go, there will not be enough.

Mom: Sorry honey. You know you are grounded and not allowed to go out for a week. I'm sure your friends can find someone else to take your place.

Anna: No, they already tried. Come on mom. You must agree that seniors need exercise and they enjoy having young people visit them.

Mom: True, but old people can't do modern dancing like you do. They like to do slow, quiet dances.

Anna: I know how to do those dances. Waltzing is easy. One, two, three… One, two, three…

9 Continue the conversation. Decide if Anna's mom will allow her to go or not.

Mom: _____
Anna: _____
Mom: _____

School Life in the United States

Read the article.

Life in an American high school is very different from the way it was in the past. For example, students are allowed to wear sneakers, T-shirts, blue jeans and even shorts to class. Boys and girls are often in the same gym class, and sometimes even play on the same basketball or football team after school. Classrooms are very informal. Students are encouraged to talk - to ask questions, to express opinions and even to disagree with the teacher. They also frequently work with other students in groups.

Forty years ago, things were different. Most schools had a "dress code", or rules about what clothes were allowed. In many places, sneakers, shorts and blue jeans were prohibited. There was usually a dress code

for teachers too, which meant that male teachers had to wear a suit and tie, and female teachers had to wear dresses. The idea of having boys and girls take gym together was unheard of. Classrooms were more formal as well. Although there would sometimes be a classroom discussion, most of

the time the teacher talked and the students listened.

Eighty years ago, there was no need for a dress code, because everyone knew they had to wear their newest and cleanest clothes to school. In many places, children from ages six to fourteen attended one room schools together. The older students would spend time teaching the younger students because the teacher couldn't teach so many different grades every day. Class work was also different. Paper and pencils were expensive, so students often did their lessons on small chalk boards at their desks. Teachers were very strict, and students did exactly what they were told to do. School life was much more formal back then.

Read the first paragraph again. Then complete the chart with ways in which your school is the same as an American high school and ways in which it is different.

Same as an American high school	Different from an American high school
Boys and girls have gym together.	We have to wear school uniform.

Write the following statement in the correct column.

	40 years ago	80 years ago
There was a dress code.	_____	_____
Several grades were in the same room.		
There were no notebooks.	_____	_____
Everyone wore their newest clothes to school.	_____	_____
Sneakers were not permitted in school.		

Review 1

Anna, Liza and Ben are visiting a senior citizen's home to give a dance class.

1 Complete the conversation using the words in the box.

did you	can we	meet
aren't we	didn't you	introduce

Superintendent: Good morning, everyone. I'd like to (1) _____ Liza, Anna and Ben. They're going to do the dance class.

Senior citizens: Hi there. Nice to (2) _____ you.

Superintendent: Okay kids. These are our star dancers, Gertie and Lance.

Gertie: We're going to do waltzes and old dances, (3)_____?

Liza: Sure. Are you looking forward to it?

Gertie: Of course! You didn't forget to bring the music, (4) _____?

Anna: Of course not. We can't dance without music, (5) _____?

Lance: You brought some nice music, (6) _____? I don't want any of that hip hop stuff.

Ben: Don't worry. The CD is called "Ballroom Dancing from the 50s".

Gertie: Now that's my kind of music.

2 Complete the interview with Gertie and Lance using information in the chart.

	Gertie	Lance
go to dance halls	✓ *(only with other girls)*	✗ *(didn't use to dance)*
allowed to go to parties	✗ *(strict parents)*	✓ *(a lot!)*
watch TV	✓ *(black and white)*	✗ *(no TV)*

Interviewer: Gertie, when you were young, did you use to go to discos?

Gertie: No, there weren't any discos in those days. I used to . . .

Interviewer: _____

Lance: _____

_____

_____

3 Write the words in parentheses in the gerund or the infinitive.

Anna: What's life like here, Gertie?

Gertie: It's good. They encourage us (exercise) 1. _____every day so we keep fit and active.

Anna: Yes, you are an excellent dancer. What else do you spend your time (do) 2. _____?

Gertie: We do art classes and yoga. I have trouble (do) 3. _____yoga though. My legs are not as flexible as they used to be.

Anna: You do yoga! Wow! I'd love (try) 4. _____that.

Gertie: Yes, and I've decided (start) 5. _____ swimming.

Anna: Great! Being old sounds like good fun!

Gertie: Yes, but there are so many rules in this place. Sometimes you feel like a kid.

4 Read the rules of the senior citizen's home. Then say if you agree with them or not and give your reasons.

> **Rules**
> a. Residents are not allowed to keep pets.
> b. Residents are not permitted to smoke inside the building.
> c. Residents are required to switch off their lights at 10:00 p.m.
> d. Residents are requested to keep quiet at all times.
> e. Residents are allowed to have only two visitors a week.

1. _I think senior citizens should be allowed to keep pets. They need something to look after._
2. _In my opinion,_ _____
3. _____
4. _____
5. _____

5 The superintendent, Miss Aisle, has to write a report every day. She doesn't use full sentences and the sentences are very short. Rewrite the report in full sentences.

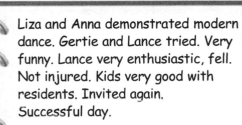

> Saturday, November 3rd
> Visit by three young people.
> Girls supervised dancing. Ben played music. Started with waltzes and foxtrots. Gertie and Lance best dancers. Others fairly good.
>
> Liza and Anna demonstrated modern dance. Gertie and Lance tried. Very funny. Lance very enthusiastic, fell. Not injured. Kids very good with residents. Invited again. Successful day.

Today we had _____
_____
_____
_____
_____
_____

6 Write the question or the answer.

1. Q: What did Ben do at the dance class?
   A: _____
2. Q: _____
   A: No, Lance didn't use to watch TV.
3. Q: _____
   A: Gertie and Lance were the best dancers.
4. Q: What happened to Lance at the dance class?
   A: _____
5. Q: Would you like to visit a senior citizen's home? Give your reasons.
   A: _____

1 Complete the conversation. Then fill in the crossword.

Ann: What would you do if you won the (6 across) _____?

Terry: I'd throw a (4 down) _____ for my friends, then I'd buy myself an (3 across) _____ watch and get myself lots of fashionable (5 down) _____. What would you do?

Ann: Well, I wouldn't (2 down) _____ all the money on myself. I would make a (1 down) _____ to a (5 across) _____ for homeless kids.

2 Match the imaginary situation with the possible action.

1. If I found a lot of money,
2. If I lost my wallet,
3. If I spoke English perfectly,
4. If I were vacationing in the USA,
5. If we didn't have classes tomorrow,

a. I would go to all the big theme parks.
b. I would stay in bed until 10:30.
c. I would buy a sports car.
d. I would get a job at the United Nations.
e. I would report it to the police.

3 Number the sentences to make a conversation.

____ Listen, nobody has long hair these days. And if they do, they wash it!

____ And if you had a more fashionable haircut, maybe you would look better.

____ What's wrong with my clothes? I like jeans and T-shirts.

____ But my hair looks cool.

____ Okay, then I'll buy some new shirts.

_1_ Hi Jim. I need some advice. The girls seem to like you. Why don't they like me?

____ Well, if you wore some smarter clothes, that would help.

____ You like jeans and T-shirts, but girls don't.

4 Write questions using the words in parentheses. Then write an answer.

1. Q: (what / you do / find / $50) <u>What would you do if you found $50?</u>
   A: <u>I would take it to the police.</u>

2. Q: (what / you do / go / USA) _____
   A: _____

3. Q: (what / parents do / you come home / 1:00 a.m.) _____
   A: _____

4. Q: (what / you do / lose / school bag) _____
   A: _____

5. Q: (what / sister do / you take / favorite CD) _____
   A: _____

6. Q: (what / you do / there is / an earthquake) _____
   A: _____

LOOK!

A common mistake is to put *would* in the *If* clause.
INCORRECT: If I *would* find $300, I would buy a digital camera.
CORRECT: If I *found* $300, I would buy a digital camera.

5 Unscramble the sentences.

1. call cell I I If lost my my number. own phone, would
   <u>If I lost my cell phone, I would call my own number.</u> _____

2. $300, a bank. check for got I I If in it put the would
   _____

3. a allowed get I If job. me, my parents part-time would
   _____

4. would won the lottery, If I I house. buy a
   _____

5. charity. give had I I If it money, more to would
   _____

6. you, would were If I I haircut. get a
   _____

6 Use the cues below to make hypothetical statements.

win / lottery	1 <u>If I won the lottery</u>, I would buy a new house for my grandmother.
not find / notebook	2 _____, you would look better.
go / coffee shop	3 _____, I would look for it at school.
turn up / late	4 _____, you would definitely pass.
cut / hair	5 _____, I would get a cappuccino.
study	6 _____, I would wait until she arrived.

LESSON B If I had an extra ticket, I'd invite you.

7 Match the words that have almost the same meaning.

1. funny
2. energetic
3. extroverted
4. introverted
5. artistic
6. boring

a. athletic
b. self-confident
c. shy
d. creative
e. dull
f. amusing

8 Read the letter and the reply in the beauty section of a teen magazine. Then answer the questions.

Dear Maggie.
I am going for a job interview as a part-time sales assistant in a big department store. I don't think I will get the job because they want people that are 18 years old and I am only 16. Also, they want attractive, slim girls and the truth is, I'm not very slim. What can I do? I have enclosed my photo.

Kim

Okay, Kim. The first thing is BE CONFIDENT. If you think you will get the job, you will get it! But here are a few ideas that might help. I think if you cut your hair, you would look older. Definitely don't wear your hair in a pony tail! Then, if you wore vertical stripes she would look thinner. This always works. Also, if you wore a red dress, you would look more self-confident. Red is a powerful color. Finally, if you put on darker make-up you would look older. Don't ask me why, but it's true!

Good luck with your interview.
I'm sure you will get the job.

Maggie

1. Why doesn't Kim think she will get the job?

_____

2. What ideas does Maggie have to make Kim look older?

_____

3. What should Kim do to look thinner?

_____

4. What other advice does Maggie give?

_____

9 Think of a someone you know who could look better. Write some advice to him or her.

If you changed your hair style, you would look better.

_____

_____

_____

_____

Flow charts

Flow charts are a map of a process. The steps in the process are represented in the chart with arrows. Flow charts help us see whether the steps in the process are logical. They are used a lot in computer programming and by people who have to make plans.

Here is a flow chart for someone who is lost in a foreign city and needs to get back to their hotel.

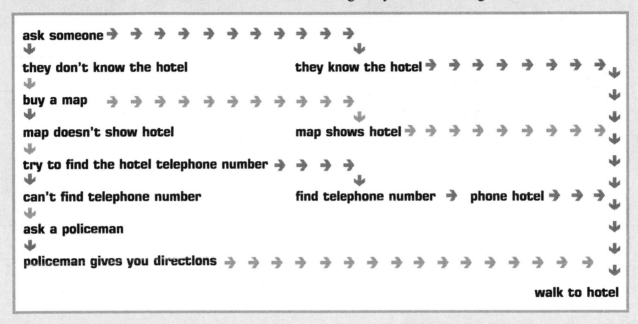

This sequence of steps can be written in every day English, starting like this:

If I were in lost in a foreign city and I couldn't find my hotel, I would ask someone.

Continue the sequence of steps.

If they didn't know,

_____

_____

_____

Here is a sequence of steps written in every day English. Write it out as a flow chart.

If I were planning a weekend trip to the mountains, I would first check the weather forecast.

If the weather forecast was bad, I would cancel the trip.

If the weather forecast was good, I would try to find a cheap hotel

If I could find a cheap hotel, I would make a reservation.

If I couldn't find a cheap hotel, I would try to find a campsite.

If I couldn't find a campsite, I would cancel the trip.

If I could find a campsite, I would invite some friends and we would go by bus.

Unit 6

It must belong to Carla.

1 **Label the pictures using the words in the box.**

bus pass	breath freshener	cell phone	lipstick
car keys	playing cards	water bottle	toothbrush

1. _____

2. _____

3. _____

4. _____

5. _____

6. _____

7. _____

8. _____

2 **Number the sentences to make a conversation.**

___ It might be Linda's.

___ No, Linda's phone is an old one and this is new.

___ Then it must belong to Susan. She definitely has a new, blue phone.

___ Well, if it's not Linda's, it may belong to Alonso.

_1_ Whose cell phone is this?

___ Yes, it might be, but I think Alonso's is blue and this one is black.

3 **Fill in the blanks with *must* or *can't*.**

1. A: This is a brand new cell phone.

   B: Then it _____ be Al's. He has an old cell phone.

2. A: This water bottle has the name Betty on it.

   B: Then it _____ belong to Betty Brown. She has a water bottle with her name on it.

3. A: This toothbrush looks just like yours.

   B: It _____ be mine. I left mine at home.

4. A: Whose iPOD ™ is this?

   B: Susan and Bill both have iPODs ™. It _____ be Bill's.

5. A: Alice lost her car keys at the soccer game.

   B: I found these on the soccer field. They _____ belong to her.

4 Complete the sentences. Use the words in the box.

must	whose
might	can't
can't	may

A common mistake is to place **to** after **must**.

Incorrect
It must ~~to~~ belong to Jean.

Correct
It must belong to Jean. /
It has to belong to Jean.

A: Whose lunch is this?

B: It (1) _____*might*_____ be Kim's. She likes chicken sandwiches.

A: No, it (2) _____be hers. She stayed home today.

B: Well, then it (3) _____be Ron's. He likes chicken.

A: No, it (4) _____be his. He had pizza for lunch.

B: I know (5) _____sandwich it is.

A: Whose?

B: It (6) _____ be Gary's. He told me he lost his lunch.

5 Read the description of the bag. Then use the information from the chart to complete the statements.

A blue bag with a CD player, a packet of potato chips, a guitar magazine and a romance novel.

A: It (1) _____ be David's. He has a blue bag

B: It (2) _____ be David's because there a romance novel in the bag.

A: It (3) _____be Ian's because his favorite snack is potato chips.

B: It (4) _____ be Ian's because his bag is green.

A: Then it (5) _____ be Carla's.

	Carla	Ian	Marina	David
Favorite snacks	potato chips	potato chips	nuts	fruit
Interests	music	soccer	iPOD ™	playing the guitar
Color of bag	blue	green	green	blue
Other contents	romance novel	pair of sunglasses	lipstick	bicycle lock

6 Use the chart in exercise 5 to write another conversation for another bag. Describe the bag first.

Description: _____

A: _____

B: _____

A: _____

B: _____

A: _____

LESSON B Could this time capsule be from 1998?

7 Complete the statements. Use the words in the box.

can't
might
could
may
must

A: Look, the time capsule has a CD by Bon Jovi called Always.

B: Well, it (1) _____ be from the 1980s. Bon Jovi wasn't around. I'm not sure but it (2) _____ be from the 1990s

A: Look, here is a picture of Pete Sampras winning Wimbledon.

B: Okay, so it (3) _____ the mid-1990s because he won Wimbledon in '93, 94 and '95.

A: And here's a photo of Tom Hanks receiving an Oscar.

B: Okay. He won back-to-back Oscars in 1994 and 1995 so the time capsule (4) _____ come from 1995.

A: Oh, look. It says it's for a film called "Forest Gump".

B: Then it (5) _____ be 1995.

8 Read the following newspaper clippings. Use clues from the clippings to answer the questions.

Newspapers are like time capsules. They contain news and information about a particular time. All these newspapers come from one particular year.

Pokemon Fever

This year was Pokémon year. First there was the video game, followed by the television show, the cards, the toys, the t-shirts, the toothbrushes and then the movie, which went straight to number one. It is hard to imagine now, but by this time next year, they might be almost forgotten.

Nelson to retire

Nelson Mandela, first black president of South Africa, steps down (June 16), and Thabo Mbeki takes over. President Mandela says he wants to spend more time on his farm but he might . . .

Movie News

Could The Phantom Menace become the film of the year?

Entertainment

The Best of the Year: "I Believe" by Cher was the best selling single of the year.

Y2K BUG ATTACK?

The world waits to see what might happen with the Y2K computer bug. Some scientists say that it could destroy all the computers in the world.

1. From what year do you think the clippings come?

_____

_____

2. What was Pokemon fever?

_____

_____

3. Who was the president of South Africa in January of this year? _____

_____

4. As well as spend time on his farm, what do you think President Mandela might do? _____

_____

Looking for Dinosaurs

Read the article.

The study of dinosaurs first began when someone uncovered a dinosaur jaw bone in Holland in 1770. Soon other dinosaur bones were discovered in England and scientists began to put the bones together to make models of dinosaurs. In 1855, Edward Drinker Cope and Othniel Charles Marsh discovered dinosaur teeth and bones in the United States and began to construct their own dinosaur models. Although they made some mistakes (such as putting the head on the wrong end of the dinosaur models), their work added greatly to our knowledge of dinosaurs. By the 1890s, these two men had discovered 130 new types of dinosaurs using bones they found in Colorado, Montana and Wyoming.

Today there are thousands of places where dinosaur bones may be found. However, there are not enough scientists to go to all these places. The Denver Museum of Natural History is helping solve this problem by training dinosaur hunters. They offer eight courses on how to find and take care of dinosaur bones. They have already graduated 100 "dinosaur hunters".

Match the words that have the same meaning.

1. uncover	a. not right
2. construct	b. discover
3. training	c. find and answer
4. solve	d. build
5. wrong	e. teaching
6. offer	f. give

Put the events in the correct order.

___ Dinosaur bones are discovered in the United States.

___ The Denver Museum of Natural History begins training dinosaur hunters.

_1_ Dinosaur bones are discovered in Holland.

___ One hundred and thirty new types of dinosaurs are discovered.

___ Dinosaur bones are discovered in England.

Write the question or the answer.

1. Q: Where was the first dinosaur bone discovered?
   A: _____

2. Q: _____
   A: It was discovered in 1770.

3. Q: What mistakes did Cope and Mash make?
   A: _____

4. Q: _____
   A: They discovered 130 new types of dinosaur.

5. Q: Why does The Denver Museum of Natural History train dinosaur hunters?
   A: _____

Unit 7 LESSON A
We need a band that's popular.

1 Check ✓ the boxes that go together, write an ✗ in the boxes that don't go together. Then write sentences that are true for you.

	play their own songs.	film their own videos.	I've seen before.	people can dance to.	play the latest hits.
I like DJs who	✓	✗	✓	✓	✓
I like movies which					
I like bands which					
I like CDs that					

1. _____
2. _____
3. _____
4. _____
5. _____

2 Complete the statements. Use the words *who* or *which*.

1. I prefer DJs _____who_____ play really loud music.

2. I don't like movies _____ have unhappy endings.

3. Nobody likes people _____ show up late.

4. It's difficult to find bands _____ will attract young people.

5. I prefer music _____ I already know.

6. Let's find someone _____ everyone knows.

3 Number the sentences to make a conversation.

<u>1</u> Hi, Connie. Have you found a DJ that is free for next Saturday?

___ You're right! Maybe I could find a DJ that plays a variety of music.

___ No, I haven't. I found a DJ who can come but not a band.

___ Really! I prefer DJs who play a variety of music. I like to talk to my friends as well as dance.

___ So, why don't we get the DJ?

___ Sounds good to me. Keep trying. See you.

___ Well, He's not very good. I prefer a DJ who plays loud dance music.

4 Join the sentences using *who* or *which*.

1. I like energetic bands. They are interesting to watch as well as listen to.

   <u>I like energetic bands which are interesting to watch as well as listen to.</u>

2. I can't stand night clubs. They are too noisy.

   _____

3. Nobody likes lazy bands. They show up late for their concerts and don't practice.

   _____

4. Top band, Mega, have a new singer. He is really cute but he can't sing!

   _____

5. I love romantic films. They make me fell sad and happy at the same time.

   _____

6. I only like top DJs. They have the very best equipment.

   _____

5 Answer the questions truthfully. Use long answers and give your reasons.

1. Do you like people who show up late?

   <u>No, I don't like people who show up late. It's bad manners to be late.</u>

2. Which do you prefer, bands that play really loud or bands that have good light shows?

   _____

3. What kind of DJs do you like?

   _____

4. Which is more important, a singer who looks good or a singer who can really sing?

   _____

5. Do you like music that you can dance to?

   _____

6 Write questions by matching the information in the columns. Then write the answer.

Singers	play hits form the 80's
Movies	make you laugh
Bands	people can dance to
Music	people can sing to

1. Q: <u>Do you like bands that play hits form the 80's?</u>

   A: <u>No, I don't. They're boring.</u>

2. Q: _____

   A: _____

3. Q: _____

   A: _____

4. Q: _____

   A: _____

5. Q: _____

   A: _____

LESSON B Karaoke is great for students who are shy.

7 A group of students have planned a school concert. Use the chart to write their decisions.

They	chose	the band the chef a place a time a type of event a charity	that who which	did the food for the Teacher's Night. was big enough. would raise a lot of money. came last year. was convenient for everybody. that helps children.

1. _They chose the band that came last year._

2. _____

3. _____

4. _____

5. _____

6. _____

8 Read the following article from the Brentwood School magazine. Underline all the relative pronouns and then write the questions or the answers.

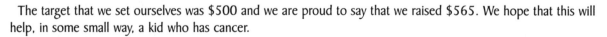

This year, the school decided to hold a Karaoke contest to raise money for children who have cancer. The event was held in the school gym and was a big success.

The contest was open to anyone who wanted to enter. This included parents, grandparents and, believe it or not, pets! Alessandra's dog, Spotty, "sang" the song "A Walk on the Wild Side" which was a howling success.

The winner of the contest was Barry from Class 7 who sang It's you I love. His parents were so happy that they gave an extra $50 to the charity. A big thank you to Mr. and Mrs. Sloan!

The target that we set ourselves was $500 and we are proud to say that we raised $565. We hope that this will help, in some small way, a kid who has cancer.

Finally, the school would like to thank all the students who helped to organize the contest. They worked very hard. Everyone who came really enjoyed themselves and we look forward to next year's contest, especially if Spotty is performing.

1. Q: Why did the school have a Karaoke contest?
   A: _____
2. Q: Did Spotty win the contest?
   A: _____
3. Q: _____
   A: The contest raised $565.
4. Q: Why did Mr. and Mrs. Sloan give $50 to the charity?
   A: _____

How does a CD work?

Read the article.

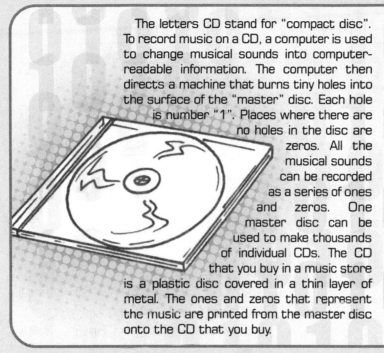

The letters CD stand for "compact disc". To record music on a CD, a computer is used to change musical sounds into computer-readable information. The computer then directs a machine that burns tiny holes into the surface of the "master" disc. Each hole is number "1". Places where there are no holes in the disc are zeros. All the musical sounds can be recorded as a series of ones and zeros. One master disc can be used to make thousands of individual CDs. The CD that you buy in a music store is a plastic disc covered in a thin layer of metal. The ones and zeros that represent the music are printed from the master disc onto the CD that you buy.

The most popular use for CDs today is to record and play back music. However, the same process is used to produce CD-ROMs. The letters CD-ROM stand for "compact disc read only memory". CD-ROMs and music CDs are almost exactly alike. However, most CD-ROMs are used to store information for use with computers, not just to hold music. One reason that CD-ROMs are so popular is that one CD-ROM can hold a lot of information. For example, a single floppy disc usually holds about 1.5 megabytes of information, while one CD-ROM can hold 630 megabytes. This allows a CD-ROM encyclopedia to include words, pictures, sound recordings, and even video scenes, making it more interesting and useful than a traditional print encyclopedia.

Match each word with a word that means the opposite.

1. individual
2. record
3. tiny
4. alike
5. buy

a. large
b. different
c. sell
d. many
e. play back

Circle the correct answers.

1. Musical sounds are recorded as ones and zeros.   True   False
2. You buy CD masters in a music store.   True   False
3. CD-ROMs and music CDs are very different.   True   False
4. CD-ROMs store information for use on computers.   True   False
5. A floppy disc holds more information than a CD-ROM.   True   False

Fill in the questions or the answers.

1. Q: CDs are used for two purposes. What are they?
   A: _____

2. Q: _____
   A: Master CDs are made by burning tiny holes into the surface of a master disc.

3. Q: Why are CD-ROMs so popular?
   A: _____

4. Q: _____
   A: CD-ROM encyclopedias are more interesting than traditional print encyclopedias because they include words, pictures, sound recordings and even video clips.

5. Q: What other ways are there of recording music?
   A: _____

Unit 8 LESSON A
After I had showered, I ran...

1 Complete the chart with the correct form of the verb.

Verb	Past tense	Past participle
1. wake up	woke up	woken up
2. leave		
3. start		
4. get		
5. meet		
6. shower		

2 Match the problems with the excuses.

Problem	Excuse
1. You didn't do your homework.	a. After I got to the Internet Café, I realized I hadn't brought the memory stick.
2. You were late for class.	b. By the time I arrived, the shop had already closed.
3. You didn't call your parents from your friend's house.	c. When I got to the bus stop, I realized I had left my bus pass at home.
4. You didn't get the shopping for your mom.	d. I suddenly remembered at 8:00 that I hadn't switched on the oven.
5. You forgot to prepare supper for your friends.	e. When I got home, I discovered I had left my books at school.
6. You didn't e-mail your assignment to your teacher.	f. By the time I realized I hadn't phoned you, it was too late.

3 Complete the sentences with words from the box below. Then number the sentences to make a conversation.

hadn't cooked

discovered

came

had forgotten

told

hadn't washed

happened

eat

___ And then I (1) _____ my brother had taken my bicycle.

___ My mom does that all the time!

___ So, did you (2) _____?

___ So, that's why you (3) _____ on the bus.

___ What a day! Everything went wrong. When I got home, my mom (4) _____ lunch.

___ Yes. And when I got off the bus, I remembered I (5) _____ my soccer boots. I'm sorry. No soccer today, I'm afraid.

___ Yes, but I had to wait an hour. Then she (6) _____ me she (7) _____ my soccer uniform.

_1_ You're late. What (8) _____?

4 Put the verb in parentheses in the correct tense.

1. I (leave) ___had left___ by the time you (arrive) _____ arrived._____

2. By the time I (be) _____ twelve, I (get) _____ tired of cartoons.

3. As soon as I closed the door, I (remember) _____ that I (leave) _____ the keys in the house.

4. By the time I (finish) _____ my homework, my favorite TV program (start) _____.

5. At 6:00, I suddenly (remember) _____ I (not do) _____ my assignment.

6. The band _____ (not arrive) by the time the concert (start) _____.

LOOK!

The time adverbs, **already** and **just** go between the auxiliary had and the past participle.

Sally had **already seen** the film.

I had **just** arrived home, when the telephone rang.

5 Unscramble the sentences.

1. eaten they supper already had
   They had already eaten supper.

2. just left Peter had
   _____

3. closed had just the shop
   _____

4. new my jeans already my Mother had washed
   _____

5. gone just up price had the
   _____

6. assignments already had teacher the collected the
   _____

6 Read the chart and the sentences. Circle True or False. Then rewrite the false sentences correctly using negatives.

Yesterday:					
3:00 p.m. have lunch	4:00 p.m. wash motorcycle	5:00 p.m. read a magazine	6:00 p.m. watch TV	7:00 p.m. do homework	8:00 p.m. walk the dog.

1. I had already washed my motorcycle at 4:00 p.m.   True   (False)
2. At 6:00 p.m., I had already walked the dog.   True   False
3. At 6:00 p.m., I watched TV.   True   False
4. At 5:00 p.m., I had already washed my motorcycle.   True   False
5. I read a magazine at 3:00 p.m.   True   False
6. I had already finished my homework at 5:00 p.m.   True   False

1. _I hadn't already washed my motorcycle at 4:00 p.m._
2. _____
3. _____
4. _____

LESSON B What happened next?

7 Complete the sentences with the correct form of the verb.

A: Did anyone play an April fool's trick on you this year?

B: They sure did! When I (arrive) 1. ___arrived___ at school, there was no-one there. My brother (change) 2. _____ my watch by one hour.

A: Nice one!

B: And that's not all. When I (go) 3. _____ to my locker, I couldn't open it. My friends (glue) 4. _____ the door.

A: What did you do?

B: I (call) 5. _____ the janitor and he opened it with a hammer.

A: So everything was okay.

B: No, My friends (take) 6. _____ all my things and (leave) 7. _____ a sign inside that said APRIL FOOL!.

8 Read the story, underline the exaggerations and then write the questions or the answers.

The Story of Paul Bunyan

Paul Bunyan was a lumberjack who lived in the far north where it was very cold, especially in winter.

One year, the winter was really cold. The rivers froze and the water turned to ice. It was so cold that when the people spoke, their words turned to ice. They spoke but no sound came out. Three months later, the spring came, the weather got warmer, and the snow and ice melted and turned to water. The words that the people had spoken in the winter, melted as well. What a noise! You could hear everything they had said in the winter three months later.

Paul had a cow called Lucy. Lucy would eat anything green - grass, leaves, even Paul's green shirt. When the winter came and snow covered all the grass and the trees, Lucy couldn't eat anything and she stopped giving milk. So, Paul made her some green sunglasses and the snow that had looked white, now looked green. Lucy ate the snow and the ice but - surprise, surprise, she didn't produce milk, she started to produce ice cream.

1. Q: _____
   A: He lived in the far north.
2. Q: Why couldn't you hear what the people said?
   A: _____
3. Q: What was Lucy's favorite color?
   A: _____
4. Q: _____
   A: No. After she had eaten the snow, she produced ice cream.
5. Q: Do you think Paul Bunyan was a real person?
   A: _____

9 Make a list of fun April fool's tricks.

_____   _____

_____   _____

April Fool's Day

Read the article.

What is April Fool's Day?

Every year on the first of April, people in many countries play jokes on each other and say things that aren't true. In France, the children stick paper fish on their friends' backs. Then they point to the fish and shout "April Fish!" In the United States a person may point to another person's shoe and say, "Your shoe's untied!" when it really isn't untied. Or a child might call a classmate in the morning before school starts and tell him or her, "There's no school today, you can stay home." In the 1800s, teachers sometimes pointed up in the sky and said, "Look at all the geese!" when there was really nothing in the sky.

When did April Fool's Day Start?

The most common answer to this question is that it began in 1582 when Pope Gregory changed the yearly calendar. Until that time, the new year began on April 1st. When the date moved to January 1st some people didn't want to change, and some just forgot about it. After that, anyone who still celebrated the new year on April 1st was called an April Fool.

Find each word in the article and guess what it means. Then write the word next to its meaning.

untied
pointed up
believe
fool
play jokes on

1. someone who isn't smart _____ fool _____

2. raised a finger towards the sky _____

3. not attached together _____

4. think _____

5. to do something which makes you laugh at someone else _____

Match the phrase to the correct date to complete the sentence.

1. Pope Gregory changed the calendar ___a___

2. There was no April Fool's Day _____

3. New Year's Day was celebrated on January 1st _____

4. The teachers fooled children _____

5. Children called each other April Fish _____

a. in 1582

b. the 1800s

c. in France

d. after 1582

e. before 1582

Write the questions or the answers.

1. Q: What is April Fool's Day?
   A: _____

2. Q: In which country do the children shout "April Fish"?
   A: _____

3. Q: _____
   A: In the United States.

4. Q: If someone phoned you on April 1st and said, "There's no school today." what would you do?
   A: _____

Review 2

1 Unscramble the sentences on the invitation.

Invitation

to invited attend a You COSTUME are PARTY,

_____

16th to my birthday. celebrate

_____

be will a costume. prize for best There the

_____

at See you party! the

_____

Ben

2 Fill in the blanks with *who* or *which*.

Ana: I want to go as a character (1) _____ is glamorous and everyone knows. Like Cinderella or a princess.

Liza: Come on! That's for kids! There won't be anyone else (2)_____is going as a fairy tale character, that's for sure!

Ana: Let me see, I'll need to find a long dress (3) _____ makes me look real elegant. And a blond wig and …..

Liza: Oh, please that's enough. I'm going to go as someone (4) _____ is really frightening, like Dracula or a witch or something.

Ana: Ugh! You can wear that horrible black dress (5) _____ you wore at the school dance.

Liza: Thank you, princess! See you at the party. Let's see (6) _____wins the prize!

3 Read the conversation between Liza and her mom. Then continue the conversation for Ana with the words in parentheses.

Liza: Mom. I have decided to go to the party as "Countess Dracula". If I tore my black dress, it would look really cool.

Mom: Okay, honey. I didn't like that black dress anyway.

Liza: And I need to do something with my teeth. Can I dye them red?

Mom: No way! You can buy some false teeth and paint them red.

Ana: (Princess Diana, your evening dress, elegant)

_____

Mom: (Yes, wear elegant dress, look like princess)

_____

Ana: (hair, cut, dye blond)

_____

Mom: (sure, buy high heeled shoes)

_____

4 Number the sentences to make a conversation.

___ It can't be! His mom is really strict. She would never let him dye his hair green and get a tattoo.

___ I don't know. It might be John.

___ No, it can't be John. John's a lot taller than that. I think it's Pablo. He's quite short.

___ Wait a minute. Ben has a tattoo on his arm just like that one. It must be Ben. It *is* Ben!

_1_ Look at that punk over there. Who do you think it is?

5 Read the e-mail. Put the verbs in the correct tense.

Message						
Accept	Reply	Forward	Delete	Print	Move to	

From: Natalia@ .net

To:

Copy:

Subject: Costume party

Attachments:

Hi Natalia,

Liza and I (have) 1. _____ a great night last night. We went to a costume party at Ben's house. Liza (decide) 2. _____ to go as "Countess Dracula", and she really looked frightening. She had bought some long false teeth that she (paint) 3. _____ red.

I went as Princess Diana. My mom allowed me to have my hair cut and dyed blond. I put on some high heeled shoes that made me look taller, and I think I looked pretty good.

When we arrived, the party (start) 4. _____ , and there were lots of people already there. Everyone (dance) 5. _____ and having a good time. Ben (dye) 6. _____ his hair green, and he was dressed as a punk. I didn't recognize him!

Ben's mom and dad were the judges for the best costume and guess who won? Liza! She (be) 7. _____ really excited and pretended to bite Ben's dad. He wasn't sure if she was serious or joking.

But—can you believe this? three different boys asked me for a date! Liza was really angry. She said that if there (be) 8. _____ another costume party, she (go) 9. _____ as a film star! Forget winning the prize.

GFI

6 Write the questions or the answers.

1. Q: What did Ben go to the party as?
   A: _____

2. Q: _____
   A: Liza won the prize for the best costume.

3. Q: _____
   A: Ben's mom and dad were the judges.

4. Q: Do you think Ben's mom and dad are strict? Why?
   A: _____

5. Q: Who do you think enjoyed the party more, Ana or Liza? Why?
   A: _____

6. Q: If you went to a costume party, who would you go as?
   A: _____

My reading journal 1

1 **Read the sentences and check True or False.**
Then rewrite the false sentences correctly.

	T	F
1. Silvia's boyfriend is called Oliver, and Oliver's father has an airplane.	☐	☐
2. Oliver's father's best friend is called Dave Norman.	☐	☐
3. Oliver's father is called Dave Norman.	☐	☐
4. Bob Drummond's wife is in business with Dave Norman.	☐	☐
5. Oliver's father and Bob Drummond were in the airplane when it crashed.	☐	☐
6. Oliver thinks someone is trying to kill Bob Drummond.	☐	☐

_____

_____

_____

_____

2 **Write sentences about the people in the story.**

Sylvia

_____

_____

_____

Oliver

_____

_____

_____

Dave Norman

_____

_____

_____

Bob Drummond

_____

_____

_____

3 **In what order did the following events happen? Number the sentences.**

___ Mr. and Mrs. Norman's car caught fire.

___ Mr. Norman and Oliver picked Sylvia up at her house.

___ Oliver and his father went for a flight while Sylvia and Bob waited in the airport diner.

___ Sylvia began to suspect that someone was trying to kill Mr. Norman.

___ Sylvia went to her Aunt Bertha's birthday party.

___ The plane crashed.

___ They drove to the airport and met Bob Drummond.

4 **How do you think the story will continue?**

_____

_____

_____

Self-check 1

1 Now I know words related to . . .

1. appearance _____
2. personality _____
3. emotions _____
4. leaning a language _____
5. organizing a school concert _____

2 Now I can make questions for these answers . . .

1. Q: _____
   A: That's right! He used to have long hair.

4. Q: _____
   A: No, I prefer bands that play quietly.

2. Q: _____
   A: No. I think teens should be in bed by 10:00
      p.m. during the week.

4. Q: _____
   A: No. By the time I arrived, the party was
      already over.

3. Q: _____
   A: Susan doesn't have an iPOD ™. It must be Bill's.

3 Now I can say ...

1. what my parents should allow me to do

   _____

2. what I would do if I were rich and famous

   _____

3. what I would do if I went to the USA

   _____

4. what type of DJ I prefer

   _____

4 Now I know how to ...

1. make small talk

   _____

2. give advice about how to look better

   _____

3. talk about learning a language

   _____

4. make excuses

   _____

Unit 9

1 Write a check mark ✓ if the words go together and a ✗ if they don't.

	someone	a bicycle	ideas	food
cheer up	✓	✗	✗	✗
fix up				
look for				
come up with				
run out of				
hand out				

2 Rewrite the sentences using the words in the box.

set up	hand out	run out of	fix up	look for	put up

1. Let's stand by the door and give the tickets to the students.
   Let's stand by the door and <u>hand out the tickets to the students.</u>

2. I hope we have enough food.
   I hope we don't _____

3. We could place some advertisements on the wall.
   We could _____

4. Why don't we paint the room and put up some pictures?
   Why don't we _____

5. Let's arrange the tables and chairs.
   Let's _____

6. Would you help me find the microphone?
   Would you help me _____

3 Answer the questions using the verbs in the box.

| cheer up |
| looking forward |
| crazy about |
| put on |
| signed up |
| turned in |

1. Are you going to join the school tutoring program?
   No, I'm not <u>crazy</u> <u>about</u> working with young kids.
2. Are you excited about going to visit the hospital?
   Yes, I'm really _____ _____ to it.
3. What are you going to do at the old people's home?
   We're going to _____ _____ a show.
4. What are you planning to do on Volunteer Day?
   I have already _____ _____ to clean the city parks.
5. Have you finished your assignment?
   Yes, I already _____ it _____ .
6. I hate doing this type of work.
   Well, _____ _____ . We'll finish soon.

4 Match the phrases to make sentences.

1. I put up
2. The teacher will hand out
3. Are you going to sign up
4. If we ran out of food
5. Let's fix up
6. I'm going to talk it over

a. that old bicycle.
b. we could buy some more.
c. a poster on my wall.
d. with my mom.
e. for Volunteer Day?
f. the papers at the end of the class.

5 Read the sentences. Complete the crossword puzzle with the correct verb phrase.

Down

1. You look sad! _____.
   Give me a smile!
2. _____ your pens. Write
   this down. It is very important.
4. You have to _____ your
   assignments by Friday. Or else!

Across

3. We go to visit my grandmother every year. I really
   _____ it. It's great fun!
5. Did you _____ to visit the hospital on
   Volunteer Day?
6. We're going to _____ the city parks this
   weekend. They are in a real mess.

Look!

For most phrasal verbs that end with *up, down, in, out, away, off,*
and *on,* we put the object pronoun between the verb and the preposition:

I fixed up my room. → *I fixed **it** up.*

For most other phrasal verbs, the object pronoun usually comes after the preposition:

I'm looking for my new shoes. → *I'm looking for **them**.*

6 Fill the gaps with phrasal verbs and object pronouns.

A: Let's tidy up the classroom. It's looking a mess. We never read these old magazines, we can
   (throw away) 1. _____ throw them away. _____

B: And these silly old games. Nobody plays with them. Let's (get rid of) 2. _____.

A: That's better. Now, what about these old posters? Why don't we (tear down) 3. _____?

B: Good idea. This is fun. I've got some new posters here, let's (put up) 4. _____

A: We need some tape or glue or something. Where is it?

B: I don't know. I'll (look for) 5. _____

A: The teacher will be happy when she sees this.

B: Yeah! It will (cheer up) 6. _____

LESSON B You could help fix up the shelter.

7 Number the sentences to make a conversation.

___ And then what would we do with the computers? Sell them?

___ But what happens if the computers are broken?

___ No. We could hand them out to old people's homes and teach the old people how to use them.

_1_ Now, I asked you to come up with some new ideas for Volunteer Day. Any ideas, Ricardo?

___ People often buy new computers every 2 or 3 years and they usually throw away the old computers. We could go around and collect the old computers

___ Tell us all about it then.

___ Well, I've come up with one idea. It may work.

___ Well, we could fix them up. I'm good with computers.

8 Read the letter, underline the phrasal verbs and then answer the questions.

> Dear Neal,
>
> We've finally decided what to do for my father's birthday. We had to come up with a way to surprise him. On my last birthday all he said was, "Get your bathing suit, Jim. We're going swimming." But then he took me to the aquarium and I swam with the dolphins. That was so great! And now my sister and I want to do something nice for him. He says he just wants to forget his birthday, but we know he really wants a party. He's been a little stressed out recently, and we want to cheer him up.
>
> So, we've called up all his friends and set up a surprise party. Instead of bringing gifts, we've asked each person to write down on a piece of paper a thing they like about my dad. My sister and I are going to make paper airplanes. Then when he comes in, we'll all throw the airplanes at him and shout "Surprise!" It will be really funny. And then we'll put them up on the wall so that everyone at the party can read them.
>
> The party is next Thursday at 8:00 p.m. I hope you can come.
>
> Sincerely,
>
> Jim

1. Did Jim forget his father's birthday?

_____

2. How has Jim's dad been feeling recently?

_____

3. What do Jim and his sister want to do for their dad?

_____

4. What are the people at the party going to do?

_____

5. What will happen to the paper airplanes after they throw them?

_____

9 Write a paragraph about a party you have been to that you enjoyed.

_____

_____

_____

Go for it!
World Hunger

Read the article.

Most of us don't think too much about world hunger. When we are hungry, we can always find something to eat - usually something delicious. But in many parts of the world - even in some rich countries - adults and children go to bed hungry every day.

According to the World Hunger Program in Newport, Rhode Island, 780 million people in the world don't get enough food to eat. One out of every six babies in the world is born underweight and even worse, one out of every three children is underweight at the age of five.

There are two main causes of hunger - food "shortage" and food "poverty". A food shortage happens when there isn't enough food in an area to feed all the people that live there. This has happened recently in some African countries when there wasn't enough rain for the people to grow the food they needed. Sometimes a food shortage affects just one part of the country, and at other times the whole country is affected. Food poverty is the cause of hunger when people don't have enough money to buy food. There is plenty of food in the stores, but some people can't afford to buy enough food, so they are hungry.

Match each word with the correct meaning.

1. underweight   a. one person
2. shortage   b. whole
3. entire   c. have enough money
4. individual   d. too small
5. afford   e. not enough of something

Scan the article and fill in the blanks.

1. At least _____ people in the world are hungry every day.
2. The World Hunger Offices are in _____.
3. _____ babies are underweight when they are born.
4. _____ are underweight at age five.
5. _____ happens when people don't have enough money to buy any food.
6. A _____ happens when there is no food in an area for people to buy.

Say if you agree or disagree with these statements. Give your reasons

1. People in counties that have enough food should eat less. Then there would be enough food for the people in the countries that don't have enough food.

   _____

   _____

2. Governments shouldn't send food to areas where there are food shortages. They should send seeds and fertilizers.

   _____

   _____

Unit 10 LESSON A
Where would you go?

1 Check ✓ the boxes that you think describe the activity. Write an ✗ in the boxes that don't go together.

	beach holiday	mountain holiday	city holiday	theme park holiday
educational				
boring				
exotic				
risky				
quiet				
overwhelming				

2 Match the phrases to make sentences.

1. If I went to the beach,
2. If we went to New York,
3. If I had a holiday in the mountains,
4. If we took a theme park holiday,
5. If I took a holiday in Australia,
6. If we didn't go on holiday,

a. we'd visit the Empire State Building.
b. I'd buy you a Euroland T-shirt.
c. I'd go scuba diving with the sharks.
d. I'd just relax.
e. we'd save a lot of money.
f. I'd like to try snowboarding.

3 Number the sentences to make a conversation.

___ And finally, I would spend about a month just relaxing on a beach in Zanzibar.

___ Are they in Africa?

___ Gee. I've never heard of Zanzibar. I guess I need to read a bit more about Africa.

___ I think I would like to go to Africa.

_1_ If you had a lot of money, where would you like to go?

___ Now, that is definitely Africa.

___ Well, I would start with the pyramids in Egypt.

___ Where would you go in Africa? It's a big place.

___ Yes, of course they are. Then I would go to the game parks in Kenya.

4 Unscramble the questions and then match each question with the correct answer.

Questions	Answers
1. What the if you went to do beach? would you _What would you do if you went to the beach?_	a. Yes! I would love to see the Eiffel Tower.
2. Where stay would you to the mountains? if went you _____	b. I would relax in the sun.
3. would you try got the chance, rock climbing? If you _____	c. No, it's too dangerous.
4. would you the chance, like to go to New If you had York? _____	d. I would stay at a ski resort.
5. enough money, like to go to If you had Europe? would you _____	e. No, I don't like big, noisy cities

5 Write questions using the words in parentheses and then write an answer.

1. Q: (if / go / beach / try / scuba diving?)
   If you went to the beach, would you try scuba diving?
   A: _No, I wouldn't. It's too dangerous._

2. Q: (If / have / enough money / where / go?)
   _____
   A: _____

3. Q: (What / do / if/ go / beach?)
   _____
   A: _____

4. Q: (try / sea kayaking / if / have / chance?)
   _____
   A: _____

5. Q: (If / get / chance / try / snorkeling?)
   _____
   A: _____

6. Q: (if / have / choice / go / to / beach /or / mountains?)
   _____
   A: _____

6 Fill in the gaps using either *actual* or *hypothetical conditionals*.

Actual Conditional	Hypothetical Conditional
1. If I go to the beach, I will just relax.	_If I went to the beach, I would just relax._
2. _____	If I went to the mountains, I wouldn't go skiing.
3. If you wear a hat, you won't get a sunburn.	
4. _____	If I went to the USA, I would visit Disneyland.
5. If you follow the instructions, you won't get hurt.	_____

LESSON B If I had known this would happen, ...

7 **Write the sentences in the hypothetical past.**

1. If I (know) it was going to rain, I (not go) to the beach.

   If I had known it was going to rain, I wouldn't have gone to the beach.

2. If you (leave) earlier, you (arrive) on time.

   _____

3. If you (give) me your passport, you (not lose) it.

   _____

4. If you (phone) last week, I (reserve) a room for you.

   _____

5. If you (check) the car, it (not break down)

   _____

8 **Write the consequences of these sentences.**

1. If you listened more carefully, you would understand the instructions.

   But you don't listen and so you don't understand.

2. If you had listened more carefully, you would have understood the instructions.

   But you didn't listen and so you didn't understand.

3. If you did your chores quickly, you would have more time to go out with your friends.

   _____

4. If had done your chores quickly, you would have had more time to go out with your friends.

   _____

5. If you drove more carefully, you wouldn't have so many accidents.

   _____

6. If you had driven more carefully, you wouldn't have had an accident.

   _____

9 **Read the situations and then give advice.**

1. Someone called you when you were out. Your brother took the call but forgot the number because he didn't write it down.

   If you had written down the number, you wouldn't have forgotten it.

2. Your sister never picks up her room and so she always loses her things.

   _____

3. Your friend spent all her money on some new ice skates, and now she has no money to go to the ice rink.

   _____

4. Your dad never does any exercise, so he is a little overweight.

   _____

5. Your friend had a skiing accident because he didn't stay with the instructor.

   _____

The Tropical Rain Forest

Read the article.

The word "tropical" refers to parts of the world where the weather is always warm. The largest tropical rain forests are found near the equator in South America, Asia and Africa. Although 70 percent of the plants in a rain forest are trees, there are many other green plants, as well as a large variety of animals and insects. In fact, there are more types of plants and animals in tropical rain forests than there are in all other parts of the world combined.

Tropical rain forests are divided in to three levels of plant life.

- The tallest plants are very large trees which may grow up to 200 feet tall. They form a sort of roof called a "canopy". However, there is always enough space between the trees so that the sun can always shine through the canopy. Many mammals, including monkeys and squirrels, live in the canopy.

- The middle level contains smaller trees which grow closer together. Some animals live at this level and never go down to the forest floor, for example the sloth. Here many different types of beautiful flowering plants, such as orchids and bromeliads, are found attached to the side of trees.

- The lowest level is the forest floor. Because little sunlight reaches this area, few plants grow here, mainly ferns. However, this is the level where you can find many insects and a few members of the cat family.

Write the words from the box in the correct column.

squirrels	ferns	very tall trees	smalltrees	flowers monkeys	cats

The canopy	The middle level	The forest floor
_____	_____	_____
_____	_____	_____
_____	_____	_____

Write the answers or the questions.

1. Q: _____
   A: No, there are no tropical rain forests in Europe.
2. Q: Are there more trees than plants?
   A: _____
3. Q: What is a canopy?
   A: _____
4. Q: _____
   A: Sloths live in the middle level.
5. Q: What animals live on the forest floor?
   A: _____
6. Q: Are there tropical rain forests in your country?
   A: _____

Unit 11

LESSON A
When was it invented?

1 Check ✓ the words that go together. Write an ✗ under the words that don't go together.

	car	airplane	song	penicillin	computer program
was invented					
was discovered					
was written					
was improved					
was made					

2 Unscramble the questions and then match them with the correct answer.

1. invented? piano When was the
   <u>When was the piano invented?</u>

2. telephone? invented the Who
   _____

3. a is for? pen used What
   _____

4. When invented? the was computer
   _____

5. are used sneakers What for?
   _____

6. CDs What for? used are
   _____

a. It was invented in 1960.

b. They are used for running.

c. It was invented in 1709.

d. They are used for recording music or storing computer data.

e. It is used for writing.

f. Alexander Graham Bell invented it.

3 Fill in the blanks using the words in the box. Some words may be repeated.

discovered	invented	made	named	used

1. X-rays were ___discovered___ by William Roentgen in 1895

2. The World Wide Web (www) was _____ by Tim Berners-Lee, in 1990.

3. The Popsicle ™ was invented by Frank Epperson. At first it was _____ the "Epsicle".

4. Computer controlled robots are _____ in the manufacture of cars.

5. Many discoveries are _____ accidentally.

48   GREAT IDEAS

4 Change the sentences from active to passive.

1. Alexander Graham Bell invented the telephone about 100 years ago.
   <u>The telephone was invented by Alexander Graham Bell about 100 years ago.</u>

2. The Chinese Emperor, Shen Nung, accidentally discovered tea.
   _____

3. Just one man, Tim Berners-Lee, created the whole World Wide Web.
   _____

4. Doctors use x-rays to diagnose illnesses.
   _____

5. A volcano completely destroyed Pompeii.
   _____

6. The introduction of seat belts reduced the number of deaths and injuries on the roads.
   _____

5 Fill in the blanks. Use the words in the box.

who	when	what

1. _____When_____ was television invented?
2. _____ invented it?
3. _____ is television used for?
4. _____ discovered penicillin?
5. _____ is penicillin used for?
6. _____ was it discovered?

6 Read the questions. Then write the answers.

1. Q: <u>When was the stove invented?</u>
   A: The stove was invented in 1896.

2. Q: _____
   A: The Wright brothers invented the airplane.

3. Q: _____
   A: The washing machine is used to wash clothes.

4. Q: _____
   A: The telephone was invented by Alexander Graham Bell.

5. Q: _____
   A: The helicopter was invented in 1939.

6. Q: _____
   A: Penicillin is used by doctors.

LESSON B The world has been changed by . . .

7 Use the information in the table to write sentences.

	who	where	used for
X-rays	Wilhelm Roentgen	Germany	taking radiograph
Superglue	Dr. Harry Coover	USA	sticking things together quickly
Penicillin	Alexander Fleming	Great Britain	treating infections.
Post-its	Spencer Silver	USA	writing notes
Writing	Olmecs	Ancient Mexico	making permanent records

1. X-rays were discovered by Wilhelm Roentgen in Germany. They are used for . . .
2. _____
3. _____
4. _____
5. _____

8 Read the passage and underline all the passives. Then answer the questions.

Our lives <u>are surrounded</u> by writing - in books, on the Internet, on TV, - everywhere! But how often do we stop and think, who invented writing? What would our lives be like if there were no writing?

Before writing was invented, all knowledge was passed from generation to generation orally. There are two problems here. First, knowledge and ideas spread very slowly; you can only get ideas from people that you actually meet. Secondly, the human memory is not perfect - facts are forgotten or changed. But writing changed all that! Now facts can be communicated accurately and rapidly to almost any other person. But who invented writing?

It is thought that writing was invented at least twice in different parts of the world. An early type of writing was invented by in the Middle East by the Sumerians in about 3200 BC. Later, in ancient Mexico, the Olmecs also invented another type of writing. In early writing, symbols were used to represent whole words, so ☾ would mean "moon". Later symbols were used to represent individual sounds.

So, the next time you pick up a magazine or a book, or switch on your computer, or write a message to your mom, say thank you to an unknown inventor who made this all possible.

1. Give some more examples of where we can find writing in our daily lives.

   _____

2. What are the problems with oral communication?

   _____

3. Symbols that represented whole words changed to symbols representing individual sounds. Why do you think this happened?

   _____
   _____

Go for it!

Discoveries and Inventions

Read the articles.

Marie Curie

Mary Curie (whose birth name was Manya Skldowska) was born in Poland on November 7th, 1867. Her father was a high school physics teacher and encouraged her interest in science. In 1891, she went to study in Paris and changed her name to the French Marie. Two years later, she passed the examination for a degree in physics with the highest grade in her class. She later married the French physicist Pierre Curie.

Marie Curie became interested in the work of Conrad Roentgen who discovered x-rays in 1895. She knew the element uranium gave off rays similar to x-rays and she wanted to find new uses for these rays. Pierre Curie stopped his own work and joined his wife in hers. In 1898, they announced the discovery of two new elements: radium and polonium, both of which gave off more rays than uranium. In 1903, she and her husband won the Nobel Prize in Physics for isolating pure radium. In 1911, Marie Curie won a Nobel Prize in Chemistry, too. Later in life, she became ill from the effects of working with radium, and died in 1934.

William S. Burroughs.

William Burroughs was born in Rochester, New York on January 28, 1857. His first job was as a bank teller at Cayuga County National Bank. He was not well, so he had to move to a warmer place and went to live in St. Louis, Missouri in 1882. Soon after he moved there, he began working on a machine that would add and subtract numbers. There were no computers or adding machines at the time, and Burroughs thought that his machine would save bank tellers a lot of time and help them make fewer mistakes.

Burroughs made his first machine in 1885, but it didn't work very well. If you pulled the handle too hard, it gave the wrong answer. By 1893, he had found a way to make the machine work well all the time. He became ill and retired from his company in 1897. Burroughs died in 1898. That year over one thousand of his adding machines were being used all over the world.

Read the article and fill in the chart.

	Marie Curie	William Burroughs
1. Place of birth		
2. Date of birth		
3. Place he/she moved to		
4. Date moved to new place		
5. Discovery or invention		
6. Age when discovery or invention made		
7. Age when he or she died		

Answer the questions.

1. Was Marie Curie an inventor or a discoverer? _____
2. Who died from the effects of their work, Curie or Burroughs? _____
3. In your opinion, whose work was the most important? Give your reasons.

_____

Unit 12

LESSON A
Could you please tell me . . .

1 Match the place with the activity.

Place	Activity
1. drugstore	a. cash a check
2. post office	b. work out
3. bank	c. buy some shampoo
4. gym	d. get a room for the night
5. tourist information booth	e. get a map of the town
6. hotel	f. post a letter

2 Rank the replies in the box from *not certain* to *absolutely certain*.

I think so.

I'm not sure.

Definitely, no!

Maybe. I'm not really sure.

Of course!

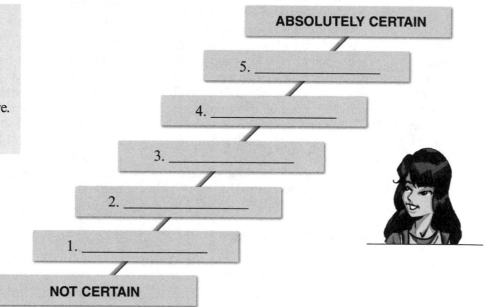

ABSOLUTELY CERTAIN

5. _____

4. _____

3. _____

2. _____

1. _____

NOT CERTAIN

3 Fill in the blanks. Then number the sentences to make a conversation.

sure	down	Excuse me	side	hand	what

___ It's about two blocks down and on the right (1) _____ side, next to the bank.

_1_ (2) _____, can you tell me where I can find a good restaurant?

___ No problem. I have lots of time. On which (3) _____ of the road is it?

___ I'm not (4) _____. Something like "La Casita".

___ Okay. I'm sure I'll find it. And (5) _____ is it called?

___ Yes, there's a good place just (6) _____ the road. They say the food is good but the service is a bit slow.

4 Write polite questions using the table. Answer the questions using the map and the prepositions in the box.

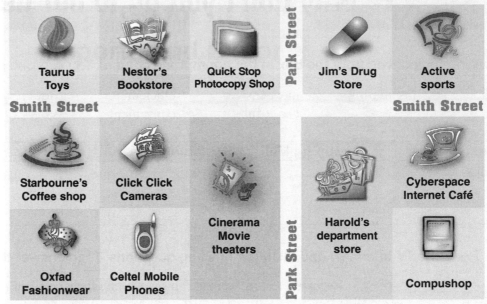

opposite				
next to	Would you mind	telling me	where	I can buy a map?
between	Will you	tell me		I can buy some shampoo?
behind	Could you	show me		I can get online?
	Can you	showing me		I can get a film?
				I can get a photo copy done?
	Do you know			I can buy a phone card?

1. Q: <u>Would you mind telling me where I can buy some shampoo?</u>
   A: <u>Sure. There's a drug store right opposite Harold's department store.</u>
2. Q: _____
   A: _____
3. Q: _____
   A: _____
4. Q: _____
   A: _____
5. Q: _____
   A: _____

5 Change the questions below into polite questions. Answer the questions using the map.

1. Q: Where's Oxfad?.
   Q: <u>Excuse me, Could you tell me where Oxfad is, please?</u>
   A: <u>Yes, it's right next to Celtel.</u>
2. Q: Where's Active Sports?
   Q: _____
   A: _____
3. Q: Where are the movie theaters?
   Q: _____
   A: _____
4. Q: Where's Active Sports?
   Q: _____
   A: _____

LESSON B Why don't you go to our newest . . .

6 Write adjectives from the box in the appropriate column. You can use some more than once.

hip	fascinating	inexpensive	efficient	not crowded	large
		beautiful	convenient	safe	

Post Office	Shopping Mall	Internet Café	Park	Dance Club
Efficient				

7 Read the TV interview and fill in the missing questions. Then answer the questions.

Reporter: Good evening. This is Karen Green reporting from Mega Mall and I have the manager James Keating here with me. Good evening, James. First, could you tell me how many stores there are in the mall?

Manager: Sure. There are 234 stores at the moment and we still have 20 vacant lots.

Reporter: That's a lot of shops! And what other attractions do you have?

Manager: Well, we have a hotel, 12 movie theaters, a water park, a .....

Reporter: Sorry to interrupt, but (1) _____ why you have a hotel in a shopping mall?

Manager: We are hoping that people will come from outside the city to visit the mall, and they will need somewhere to stay.

Reporter: I see. (2) _____

Manager: There are lots of things for young people to do. We have an amusement park with lots of rides, the movie theaters, of course, and two dance clubs.

Reporter: It sounds like there's enough to keep you busy for days. Now, I see why you need a hotel. Thanks a lot James. This is Karen Green, WSTV, Mega Mall.

1. How many stores are there in the mall?

_____

2. What other attractions are there in the mall?

_____

3. Why does the mall need a hotel?

_____

4. If you were the manager, what special events would you have organized for the opening?

_____

8 Imagine a new theme park has opened in your town. Write an interview with the manager. Use exercise 7 to help you.

_____

_____

_____

_____

Go for it!

Shopping Malls

Read the article.

Almost every major city throughout the world has at least one shopping mall. But where did they come from, and why are they such a world-wide success?

In the middle of the 20th century, as American towns and cities grew, housing in the center of towns became expensive, parking was a big problem, and many city centers became dangerous. So, the American suburb was invented. Miles and miles of low-priced houses were built outside the cities, and people then traveled in to the cities to work and to shop. Life in the suburbs was inexpensive and safe but the planners forgot one thing. Traditional towns and cities have places where people can meet and socialize: the town square, the street market, the fairground, but the suburbs had none of these. The planners hadn't provided a social focus but very soon one appeared without any planning - the shopping mall.

Downtown shop owners soon realized that if they moved their shops to the suburbs, the rents would be cheaper, and there would be lots of space for parking. Cinemas and restaurants followed the shops and before long the shopping mall was born. The shoppers who lived in the suburbs now had a safe place to shop but also a place to meet, to eat, and to be entertained.

Malls have become especially popular with teenagers around the world for many reasons. They can meet in all types of weather. They are safe. There is no entrance fee, and there is food and entertainment all under one roof. So, the shopping mall which started life in the American suburbs to meet commercial needs, has evolved in to an international social success.

Match the words in the first column with words of similar meaning in the second column.

1. suburbs   a. cheap
2. realize   b. international
3. low-priced   c. know
4. world-wide   d. city center
5. downtown   e. outside the city
6. before long   f. amused
7. entertained   g. soon

Read the passage again and fill in the chart.

ADVANTAGES FOR SHOP OWNERS

_____
_____
_____

ADVANTAGES FOR TEENS

_____
_____
_____

Answer the questions.

1. Why did people move from downtown areas to the suburbs?

2. What did the planners forget when they designed the suburbs?

3. Was the shopping mall originally intended to be a social center for teenagers?

4. What are the disadvantages of socializing in shopping malls?

Review 3

1 Read the conversation. Fill the gaps using the words in the box.

came out	help you out	fixed it up	cheer up	look for

Ana: (1) _____, Ben. What's the matter Ben? You look unhappy.

Ben: Yeah. My bike was stolen.

Liz: Oh no! What happened?

Ben: I left it outside the Internet Café and when I (2) _____, it was gone!

Ana: Oh no. And you had just (3) _____. It was looking great.

Liz: Let's go (4) _____it.

Ana: Sure. We'll (5) _____.

2 Here is some advice for Ben from the girls. Write the verbs in the correct tense.

1. If you (lock)_____it, it wouldn't have been stolen.

2. I (not leave) _____ it unlocked in future, if I were you.

3. If you (take) _____it into the café, it would have been safer.

4. If you had walked to the café, it (be) _____better.

5. If I (be) _____ you, I (go)_____ to the police.

3 Read the conversations. Then match the sentences with the location.

____ 1. **Ana:** Okay. What shall we do? I think we should go to the police.   a. at the gym

____ 2. **Ben:** No, the police are too busy to look for a bike. What about checking out the gym? There are always lots of bikes there.

____ 3. **Ana:** Wow, you're right. There are lots of bikes here. Can you see yours Ben?   b. outside the bike shop

____ 4. **Ben:** No, it's not here. What about the bike shop? Sometimes people try to sell stolen bicycles.

____ 5. **Ben:** Excuse me. Has anyone tried to sell you a blue Starider?   c. outside the Internet café

____ 6. **Shop Owner:** Sorry, kid. We don't usually buy bikes from people.

____ 7. **Ana:** Did you look through the back door of the shop? I'm sure I saw your bike, and they were painting it red.   d. in the bike shop

____ 8. **Ben:** Okay. I think it's time to go to the police.

4 The police need some information from Ben. The questions below are very direct. Rewrite these questions more politely. Use the words in the box.

could you	would you	would you mind	will you

1. Fill in this form.
   Would you mind filling in this form?

2. What does the bike look like?
   _____

3. What happened?
   _____

4. Where did you leave the bicycle?
   _____

5. Where did you find the bicycle?
   _____

5 These sentences will be used in a newspaper report. Rewrite them in the passive.

1. Mr. Alvarez left his bicycle unlocked outside the Internet Café.
   The bicycle was left unlocked outside the Internet Café.

2. It appears that a local bike shop owner's son, Glen, stole the bike.
   _____

3. He took the bike to his father's shop, where he repainted it.
   _____

4. Mr. Alvarez discovered the bicycle at the shop.
   _____

5. The court fined Glen $50.
   _____

6 Write the questions or the answers.

1. Q: Where did Ben leave his bicycle?
   A:_____

2. Q:_____
   A: No, the bike wasn't locked.

3. Q: Did Ben and Ana find the bike at the shop or at the gym?
   A: _____

4. Q: _____
   A: No, Ben didn't see the bike. Anna saw it.

5. Q: Do you think Glen should go to prison or is a $50 fine okay?
   A: _____

LESSON A
It's considered polite to bow.

1 **Match the columns.**

1. shake	a. both cheeks
2. arrive	b. your head
3. bow	c. a gift
4. kiss	d. hands
5. wear	e. on time
6. take	f. a tie

2 **Fill in the blanks using the words in the box.**

considered	expected	okay	should never	supposed	customary

1. You're _____expected_____ to make a noise when you eat noodles.

2. It's _____ rude to talk with your mouth full.

3. You _____ point with your chopsticks.

4. It's _____ to shake hands.

5. You're _____ to kiss the person on the cheek.

6. It's _____ to give your seat to an older person.

3 **Fill in the blanks with words from the box. Then number the sentences to make a conversation.**

used	mind	need	looks	year	bow
there	put	start	think	supposed	sounds

___ Well, I'm just going for two weeks on holiday, but I would like to know the customs of the country.

___ Sure. I was (1) _____ for about a (2) _____.

___ You sort of (3) _____ your hands together in front of your face and (4) _____ your head.

___ Okay. Well let's (5) _____ with meeting people. It's very different. You are (6) _____ to give a *wai* to people who are older than you.

___ That (7) _____ easy. I (8) _____ I can do that.

_1_ Hi, Pete. I really (9) _____ to talk to you. You (10) _____ to live in Thailand, didn't you?

___ It's not as easy as it (11) _____, but the Thais are wonderful people, and if you get it wrong they won't (12) _____.

___ What's a *wai*?

4 Unscramble these sentences.

1. food. much not supposed take to too You're
   You're not supposed to take too much food.

2. are chopsticks. eat expected to with You

3. It's bread eat hands. okay to with your

4. You a cheek. kiss never on person should the

5. a considered person. rude to touch It's

6. always hat house. You inside off should take the your

5 Write the answers using the words in parentheses.

1. Q: Should I kiss someone when I meet them?
   A: (kiss) No, you shouldn't kiss them.
   A: (shake hands) You should shake hands with them.

2. Q: What are you supposed to take as a gift?
   A: (food) ——————————
   A: (flowers) ——————————

3. Q: What are you supposed to wear?
   A: (jeans and sneakers) ——————————
   A: (suit and tie)——————————

4. Q: How am I supposed to eat noodles?
   A: (with a fork)——————————
   A: (with chopsticks) ——————————

6 Write the questions.

1. Q: Are you supposed to give your seat to an older person?
   A: Yes, you are supposed to give your seat to an older person.

2. Q: ——————————
   A: No, you are not expected to arrive on time.

3. Q: ——————————
   A: No, it is not considered polite to eat in the street.

4. Q: What ——————————
   A: You are supposed to take a small gift of white flowers.

5. Q: What ——————————
   A: You are expected to wear a long sleeved blouse.

LESSON B They hadn't expected me to be early.

7 Write sentences using the expressions in the box and the information in the table.

You are (not) supposed / expected to . . .
It's (not) considered rude / polite to . . .

It's (not) okay / acceptable / customary to . . .
You should (always / never) . . .

	Thailand	USA	Mexico
1. wear shorts in public	X	✓	✓
2. open gifts immediately	X	✓	✓
3. greet any woman with a kiss	X	X	✓

1. _In the United States and Mexico, it is okay to wear shorts in public. However, in Thailand_
   you should always wear long trousers in public.

2. _____

   _____

3. _____

   _____

8 Read the article and answer the questions.

What's polite in Turkey?

In Turkey, when you are invited to a friend's house, you are supposed to bring a small gift of some sort, like flowers or candy. But if you bring flowers, you are supposed to bring an uneven number, say seven or nine flowers. Never bring an even number like six or eight.

At your friend's house, you will not be given anything to eat or drink during the first fifteen or twenty minutes. In Turkey, you aren't supposed to give snacks when people arrive because it might look like you wanted them to eat and drink and then leave immediately.

When you leave, you are supposed to say good-bye several times. The first time may be before you put your coat on. The second time you may be standing just inside the door. The third time you may be outside the door. Sometimes people may even walk a little way outside the house and then say good-bye again.

1. In Turkey, would you give someone ten flowers as a gift? Give your reasons.

   _____

2. Would it be okay to take a box of chocolates?

   _____

3. Why aren't you supposed to give snacks to people when they arrive?

   _____

4. Would it be impolite to say good-bye five times?

   _____

5. What type of gifts are acceptable and which are not acceptable in your country?

   _____

Go for it!
Imports and Exports

Most countries in the world do not produce all the food they need to support their people. Therefore they import food from other countries. Many countries produce more of certain types of food than they need, so they export some food. The import and export information below is in metric tons.

Wheat Exporters

1996		2000	
United States	31, 150,000	United States	25,782,000
Canada	16, 520,000	Canada	17,658,000
Australia	14, 568,000	France	15,621,000

Wheat Importers

1996		2000	
China	9,194,000	Brazil	7, 453, 000
Brazil	7,664,000	Iran	6, 245, 000
Italy	6,262,000	Egypt	6, 050, 000

Rice Exports

1996		2000	
Thailand	5,454,000	Thailand	6,549,000
United States	2,640,000	Vietnam	3,370,000
India	2,491,000	India	2,951,000

Rice imports

1996		2000	
Indonesia	2,150,000	Indonesia	1,500,000
Philippines	867,000	Philippines	1,100,000
Brazil	792,000	Brazil	1,250,000

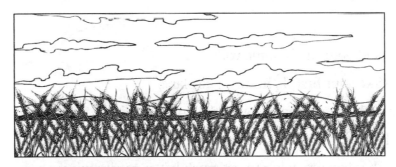

Study the charts and then answer the questions.

1. Which country exports most wheat?_____

2. In 1996, which country imported the most wheat? _____

3. Was China one of the top three rice importers in 2000?_____

4. Did Brazil import more or less wheat in 2000 than it did in 1996?_____

5. How many metric tons of rice did Thailand export in 2000?_____

6. Have Brazils imports of rice grown?_____

7. Which country is the world's largest importer of rice?_____

8. Was the USA one of the top three exporters of rice in 2000? _____

Research the figures for the present year on the Internet and write some comparisons.

LESSON A
I'm really excited about . . .

1 **Write the words in the box in the correct column.**

annoyance   boredom   confusion   determination   embarrassment   excitement
satisfaction   worry   happiness   sadness   anger   fright   tension

Positive Emotions

_____

_____

_____

_____

_____

_____

Negative Emotions

_____*annoyance*_____

_____

_____

_____

_____

_____

2 **Match the situation and the emotion**

Situation

1. Your pet cat died.

2. You don't understand your math homework.

3. You are going to take your first flight on an airplane.

4. Your kid brother is always running around the house making a lot of noise.

5. You broke your dad's new camera, and he is going to be really angry.

6. You have decided that you are going to get much better grades this year.

Emotion

a. confusion

b. worry

c. sadness

d. determination

e. excitement

f. annoyance

3 **Fill in the gaps in the conversation using one of the words in parentheses.**

A: That was the most (boring / bored) 1. _____program I have ever seen!

B: Really, I was (fascinating / fascinated) 2. _____. The bit about the dolphins was really (interesting / interested) 3. _____.

A: No, I was very (disappointing / disappointed) 4. _____.

B: But surely, you must have thought the bit about the sharks was (frightening / frightened) 5. _____?

A: No, I was just (boring / bored) 6. _____. Tomorrow it's my turn to choose, okay?

4 Complete the crossword by changing the adjectives to emotions.

Adjectives	
Across	**Down**
1. boring	2. embarrassing
5. happy	3. tense
6. angry	4. frightened
7. satisfied	7. sad
9. determined	8. worried
10. annoyed	

5 Rewrite the sentences using participle modifiers.

1. I write with my left hand.
   I am ___left handed___ .
2. I have blond hair, but my sister has dark hair.
   I have blond hair, but my sister is _____.
3. My mom works really hard.
   My mom is really _____.
4. My kid sister is a bit annoying, but she has a real sweet nature .
   My kid sister is a bit annoying, but she is really _____.
5. My dad gets really moody, but my mom has a very even temper.
   My dad gets really moody, but my mom is very _____.

Look!

Many participle modifiers don't literally mean what they say.

For example, **hot headed** doesn't literally mean someone has a 'hot head'. It means they get angry quickly.

6 Match the participle modifiers with their meaning.

1. warm-hearted
2. strong-minded
3. thin-skinned
4. shortsighted
5. tightfisted
6. narrow-minded
7. half-hearted

a. someone who does not like to spend money.
b. someone who has old fashioned ideas and ignores new ideas.
c. someone who is generous and kind.
d. someone who has strong, firm opinions.
e. someone who only plans for the immediate future.
f. someone who is very sensitive and gets hurt emotionally very easily.
g. someone who does something without much enthusiasm.

LESSON B **All those ads are just confusing.**

7 **Change the emotion in parentheses to an adjective.**

A: No one can say that Formula 1 is (boredom) 1. _____. It's the most
   (excitement) 2. _____ sport on TV.

B: Exciting! It just makes me (annoyance) 3. _____.

A: What's (annoyance) 4. _____ about it?

B: It's not about sport. It's all about advertising. Those cars are just high speed TV commercials.

A: No, the ads make the cars look more (interest) 5. _____ .

B: Well, they don't interest me! I prefer advert-free sports events, like the Olympics.

8 **Read the following passage and answer the questions.**

Advertising and the Olympic Games

In recent years, the amount of advertising in sport has increased dramatically. Advertising has brought much-needed money to sport, and because many sports have world-wide television audiences, advertisers are able to reach millions of potential customers. Stadiums are full of billboards, soccer players' clothes are covered in advertisements and there are even hot air balloons with sponsor's names above the stadiums.

However, the Olympic Games are different because they do not allow advertising in arenas or on athletes' clothing. Or are they?

There were eleven major sponsors for the 2004 Olympic Games in Athens and they paid over a billion dollars to the Games. So what did they get for their money? Well, if you wanted to eat a hamburger at the games, you could only eat the hamburgers made by the sponsor. If you wanted to wear a T-shirt with the name of a company that didn't sponsor the games, you were not allowed in to the stadium. All the billboards around the stadiums were reserved for the sponsors. Also, most people watch the Olympic Games on TV and almost all TV stations have ads. If you had watched all the Olympic Games on the TV in the USA, you would have seen about 14,000 TV commercials during the games.

So, who says the Olympic Games are different from other sport events?

1. Why does sport need advertising?
   _____

2. Why do advertisers spend money on sport?
   _____

3. Give some examples of advertising in sport.
   _____

4. In what way did the sponsors control the freedom of the individual at the Olympic Games?
   _____

5. In your opinion, do you think that advertising in sport is a good thing?
   _____

Go for it!
What Color Is It?

∿∿∿∿∿∿∿∿∿∿∿∿∿	〜〜〜〜〜〜〜
red light (long wavelength)	**violet light** (short wavelength)

Sometimes when we look at the sun high in the sky, it looks yellow. Other times, such as at sunrise and sunset, it looks red. Sometimes the sky looks blue, but other times it may appear pink or gray. Grass with the sun shining on it looks green, but in the shadow of a tree the same grass may look dark green. What is color and why do colors change?

A beam of light isn't a single straight line. Instead, light travels in waves. The length of a wave of light is called its 'wavelength'. Different colors of light have different wavelengths. For example, red has a long wavelength, while violet has a much shorter wavelength. The colors of the 'spectrum', arranged from longest wavelength to shortest wavelength, are red, orange, yellow, green, blue, indigo, and violet.

Color is the ability of the eye to notice these different wavelengths of light. The wavelengths of light an object 'reflects' and 'absorbs' give the object its color. When something absorbs one color of light, it takes that color in like a towel takes in water. When a color is absorbed by an object, that color isn't seen by the eye. When an object reflects a color, that color isn't absorbed. In this case, the color travels from the object to the eye.

For example, an apple is an object that reflects only red light. Therefore, red is the only color the eye will see. At the same time, the apple will absorb, or take in, all the other colors—orange, yellow, green, blue, indigo, and violet—and we won't see any of the colors on the apple.

Circle the correct answers.

1. Red light has a short wavelength.	True	False
2. Violet light has a short wavelength.	True	False
3. There are seven colors in the spectrum.	True	False
4. 'Reflects' means the same as 'absorbs.	True	False
5. When a color is absorbed, it isn't seen by the eye.	True	False
6. A red apple absorbs red light.	True	False
7. A red apple reflects green light.	True	False
8. Color is the ability of the eye to reflect light.	True	False

Read the word pairs. Check the appropriate column.

		same meaning	opposite meaning
1. look	appear		
2. red	violet		
3. reflect	not absorbed		
4. see	notice		
5. straight	wave		
6. take in	absorb		

Unit 15

LESSON A
Weren't you going to water the plants?

1 Check ✓ the words that go together. Write an ✗ for the words that don't go together.

	doors	refrigerator	suntan lotion	film	room
pack					
get					
lock					
clean					

2 Match the phrases to make a sentence.

1. I was going to feed the dog,   a. but it started to rain.

2. Annie was going to water the garden,   b. until we told them it was free.

3. Nobody was going to come,   c. but he never showed up.

4. The taxi was going to come at 5:00 p.m.,   d. but there was no food.

5. My brother was going to meet us at the airport,   e. but I couldn't find the key.

6. I was going to lock the garage,   f. but it was two hours late.

3 Complete the sentences with words from the box. Then number the sentences to make a conversation.

couldn't	weren't	going
was	do	Look
going		isn't

___ It's not working, but you could still pick up all the clothes on the floor. And (1) _____ you going to lock the garage?

___ There (2) _____ no soap.

_1_ Okay. Let's check everything. You were (3) _____ to tidy up your room first, then lock the garage and last, do the dishes. Did you (4)_____ everything?

___ (5) _____! It's there on the wall with the other keys. And what about the dishes?

___ Well, almost. The problem is that the vacuum cleaner (6) _____ working.

___ Well. You see, I (7) _____ find the key.

___ There's plenty under the sink. Let's hurry. We're (8) _____ to be late.

4 Write sentences using information from the notes.

	empty trash cans	water plants	clean refrigerator	tidy up kitchen	pay bills	clean garage
Mom	✓		✓			
Dad					✓	✓
Michelle		✓		✓		
David		✓				✓

1. Mom was going to empty the trash can and clean the refrigerator.
2. _____
3. _____
4. _____
5. _____
6. _____

5 Write the questions.

1. Q: Factual question - (lock garage) Were you going to lock the garage?
   A: Yes. I was, but I can't close the door.
2. Q: Surprise - (come by bus)_____
   A: Yes. We were, but it broke down.
3. Q: Checking - (David homework before supper)_____
   A: Yes, he was. Maybe he forgot.
4. Q: Factual question - (go to beach)_____
   A: No, we weren't. We decided to stay at home this year.
5. Q: Reminder - (feed the dog)_____
   A: Yes, I did. You already asked me three times!
6. Q: Factual question - (Sally buy tickets) _____
   A: Yes. She was, but it seems that she forgot.

Negative interrogatives are used when the speaker already knows the answer. So they are used for checking, to show surprise or as reminders:

Dad: *Steve, weren't you going to do your homework before you went out?*

The normal interrogative is used when the speaker doesn't know the answer. It is a factual question.

Dad: *Were you going to do your homework before you went out?*

6 Complete the sentences using the words in the box.

would
could
might
couldn't
wouldn't

1. I wanted to call you but I _____couldn't_____ find my phone card.
2. We wanted to go somewhere which _____ cost too much.
3. You're here, at last. I was wondering if you _____ come at all.
4. The sky looked dark, and we were wondering if it _____ rain.
5. I thought I _____ finish by 3:00 p.m., but unfortunately I _____.

LESSON B I was going to sign up for football, but ...

7 Write excuses using the words in parentheses.

1. Plan: Weren't you going to call me last night?

Excuse: (no telephone card) _I'm sorry. I was going to, but I didn't have a telephone card._

2. Plan: Weren't you going to visit your grandmother this afternoon?

Excuse: (bicycle chain broken)_____

3. Plan: Weren't you going to wash the dishes before your dance class?

Excuse: (finish assignment) _____

4. Plan: You're late! I thought you were going to be here at 9:00 p.m.

Excuse: (wash hair) _____

5. Plan: Weren't you going to help your dad wash the car?

Excuse: (raining) _____

8 Read the following passage. Underline examples of future in the past and circle examples of true future. Then answer the questions.

Ann and Jim have just come back from a day at the Weekend for Teens program. The idea of the program is to give teens something interesting and exciting to do at the weekend.

Jim: Hey Ann! Looks like you went to the tie-dying class. I thought you were going to sign up for the Formula 1 racing simulator.

Ann: Yes. I was going to, but you should have seen the line. There were hundreds of kids there. So, I decided to do the tie-dying.

Jim: And how was it?

Ann: Well, I imagined it might be a bit boring, but it was great! Look, I made this T-shirt.

Jim: The T-shirt is great, but your mom's not going to be happy with your green hands.

Ann: It will come off in a few days. No problem. But, what about you? You were going to go to the science museum, weren't you?

Jim: That's right. They said there was going to be a top scientist there but he never showed up.

Ann: Oh no. So, what happened?

Jim: Well, Mr. Wright, the science teacher from school, took us round. I thought it was going to be just like school, but he was really interesting. Completely different from school!

Ann: So, are you going to go back next weekend?

Jim: Sure. I'll see you at the Formula 1. But get there early!

1. How did Jim know Ann went to the tie-dying?

_____

2. Why didn't Ann go to the Formula 1 racing?

_____

3. What happened at the science museum?

_____

4. What are Ann and Jim planning to do next weekend?

_____

5. Would your mom be angry if you came home with green hands? Why?

_____

Go for it!

Saving the Temples of Abu Simbel

Read the article.

In 1960, Egypt began construction of a huge dam on the Nile river to produce electricity for millions of people. The dam, named Aswan High Dam, is about 365 feet high and over 3,000 feet across. It was completed in 1970 and cost more than a billion dollars. The lake produced by the dam was named Lake Nasser in honor of Egyptian president Gamel Abdel Nasser. The lake is more than 300 miles long and 10 miles wide.

In 1958, when the Egyptian government began to plan the dam, they realized that a very important site, the Temples of Abu Simbel would soon be lost under the waters of Lake Nasser. The temples, built over 3000 years ago, included several large and very beautiful buildings which contained statues of gods and goddesses and their children. In 1959, Egypt started working with several international groups, including the United Nations, to raise money to save the temples. Together they raised $36 million and the temples were moved to their present site, 210 feet above the level of Lake Nasser, in 1964. Today the temples are visited by many thousands of people each year. These visitors enjoy the beauty of these ancient temples and are also reminded of what international cooperation can accomplish today.

Find these words in the article. Then match each word with the correct meaning.

1. huge	a. made
2. produced	b. world-wide
3. realized	c. very large
4. international	d. get
5. raise`	e. understood
6. site	f. working together
7. cooperation	g. very old
8. ancient	h. place

Fill in the time line.

1958	1959	1960	1964	1970
Egyptian government realized Abu Simbel would . . .				

Answer the questions

1. Why was the Aswan High Dam built?

_____

2. Why do you think the Egyptian government asked international groups for help?

_____

3. Which was more expensive, building the dam or moving the temples?

_____

4. Which, in your opinion, is more important, a new dam or old temples? Give your reasons.

_____

LESSON A
It's people like us who can help.

1 Match the actions and the reasons.

Action

1. Bring your own bags when shopping and avoid using plastic bags.
2. Turn off the lights when you leave a room.
3. Walk or ride instead of driving.
4. Recycle books and paper.
5. Don't leave faucets dripping.
6. Use environmentally-friendly soap and shampoo.
7. Don't litter in public places.
8. Separate your trash.

Reason

a. It saves water.

b. It reduces the amount of plastic in the environment.

c. It saves gasoline and reduces air pollution.

d. It saves paper, and trees don't have to be cut down.

e. It looks a mess, and someone has to clean it.

f. It saves electricity.

g. It makes it easier for the authorities to recycle waste.

h. Normal soaps contain chemicals which can harm the environment.

2 Number the sentences to make a conversation.

____ But will they listen to two kids who are too young to even vote?

_1_ Don't you think we should be doing something more about environmental problems, like recycling or something?

____ Great idea! It's worth trying. Let's go for it!

____ But it's governments and big businesses that are to blame. They're the people who should be doing something.

____ Maybe they won't, but if we get some more kids to join us, maybe they would do something.

____ Oh, there are lots of kids. Let's put up some posters in the school and form a Green Club.

____ Well, if more people wrote to them and complained, maybe they would do something.

____ Okay. Who do we know who might be interested?

3 Write sentences from the chart.

I think I believe I'm sure	people businesses teens individuals governments	who which	litter ignore the warning signs don't recycle leave faucets running don't have a "green policy"	are to blame. are responsible. are at fault. are the problem.

1. _I think governments which ignore the warning signs are the problem._
2. _____
3. _____
4. _____
5. _____
6. _____

4 **Read the conversation and fill in the gaps using** *which, who* **or** *whose*.

Maria: I was reading about all the chemicals
(1) _____ farmers put on vegetables. It's disgusting. I'm not sure I want to eat vegetables ever again. But what can we do?

John: Well, you could buy from farmers
(2) _____ vegetables don't contain chemicals. You know, organic vegetables.

Maria: But there are hardly any shops
(3) _____ sell them and they are so expensive.

John: True. So why don't we grow our own organic vegetables?

Maria: But I don't know anything about growing vegetables.

John: I know someone (4) _____ can help. My father has a friend (5) _____ grows organic vegetables

Maria: But where? I live in an apartment
(6) _____ has no garden.

John: We could start an organic vegetable garden in the school. Just think, we could even sell the vegetables and make money.

5 **Unscramble the questions and write the answers.**

1. Q: you Who is do think for problems? environmental responsible
   Q: _Who do you think is responsible for environmental problems?_
   A: _I think governments because they need to make stricter laws_

2. Q: can What individuals do about saving the environment?
   Q: _____
   A: _____

3. Q: If politician, were a you you would do? what
   Q: _____
   A: _____

6 **Rewrite the sentences starting with** *It's*.

1. The kind of people who annoy me are the ones who litter parks.
   It's people who litter parks that annoy me.

2. The cars that are to blame are the ones that use a lot of gasoline.
   _____

3. The people who really bother me are the ones that play loud music late at night.
   _____

4. The people who I like are the ones who do something positive about pollution.
   _____

5. Businesses that put profit before the environment are the ones that I can't stand.
   _____

6. The governments that I admire are the ones that take alternative energy seriously.
   _____

LESSON B It's individuals who are to blame.

7 Write the words in the correct column. Some words can be used in more than one column. Then add some more words of your own.

cigarette smoke   loud music   large trucks   graffiti   gas guzzlers

litter   soap and shampoo   factories

Noise pollution	Air pollution	Visual pollution	Water pollution

8 Read the article. Underline the relative pronouns. Then answer the questions.

Clean City Air

Every year more and more people who live in the country are moving in to cities to find work. For example, the number of people who live in Bogotá, Colombia, grew by 37% between 1980 and 1990. As these people earn more money, they buy cars, and it is cars that are responsible for 80% of pollution in cities.

So, what are the authorities and big business doing about it? It seems to be impossible to slow down the growth of large cities. The only solution is to reduce the amount of pollution that is produced by the cars. Oil companies are now producing gasoline that is cleaner and produces less pollution. City authorities are providing better public transport systems, like underground trains and better bus services that encourage people to leave their cars at home.

But what can individuals do? Firstly, we should actually use the public transport systems that governments provide. Secondly, have you noticed how many cars have just one person in them? If people shared their cars, this would dramatically reduce the number of cars on the road. Finally, we could all go out and buy a bicycle. That way we would reduce the amount of pollution and get fit at the same time.

1. Why do people move from the country to cities?

2. What is the major cause of air pollution in cities?

3. What are oil companies doing about air pollution?

4. What are the authorities doing about air pollution?

5. There are three things that individuals can do. Which do you think is the best? Give your reasons.

9 Write a list of things that you are going to do to save the planet.

I am going to buy organic vegetables.

Go for it!

Endangered Species

Read the article.

Right now, over 19,000 species (or types) of plants and 5,000 species of animals are in danger of disappearing forever from the earth. When a certain species is going to disappear soon, it is called an "endangered species". When the very last one of a certain species dies, we say that the species is "extinct". Once a plant or animal is extinct, it will never appear on earth again.

There are two very important reasons why so many species are becoming endangered and extinct. The main one is that their habitats are being destroyed and they have nowhere to live. In the 20th century, man has destroyed many plant and animal habitats by building roads, houses and factories, by cutting forests and by building dams for electrical power. Another reason for the rise in the number of endangered species is the pollution caused by factories, oil spills, overuse of chemicals, and the exhaust from millions of cars.

The number of plant and animal species becoming extinct every year is growing rapidly. From 1800 until 1900, about one species per year died out. But by 1920, this had increased to about 1000 and by 1980 about 12,000 species were disappearing each year. At the end of the 20th century the extinction rate was 25,000 species per year. Scientists think that in 2020, as many as 50,000 species per year may die out. One of the biggest problems facing the earth in the 21st century is finding a way to save as many endangered species as possible.

Match each item in the first column with an example in the second column.

1. habitat
2. extinct
3. pollution
4. endangered species
5. destruction of animal habitat

a. exhaust from cars
b. dinosaurs
c. the ocean
d. the manatee
e. The Aswan High Dam

Answer the questions.

1. Do you think birds are endangered species? Why?

_____

_____

2. Which is the most important reason for many plants and animals becoming endangered or extinct?

_____

_____

3. What are the causes of pollution?

_____

_____

4. What do you think individuals can do stop animals becoming extinct?

_____

_____

Fill in the following graph using the information from the article.

Species Extinctions Since 1800

Extinctions: 60000, 50000, 40000, 30000, 20000, 10000, 0

Date: 1800 1830 1860 1890 1920 1950 1960 2010 2040

Review 4

1 Read the conversation. Then fill in the blanks with the correct verb tense.

Every year, Highbury School invites a group of students from another country to study for one semester. Last year, they invited a group of students from Indonesia, and this year they have invited a group of Thai students.

Anna: Do you remember last year when the Indonesian students were here?

Ben: Yes, we had to change our plans several times because we (not study)
1. _____ their customs before they came.

Liz: That's right. We (take) 2. _____ them to the beach, but then we found out that some girls (not wear) 3. _____ bathing suits. So we decided to take them to the mall instead.

Anna: Yes, and then we (go) 4. _____ to take them to visit my Grandma, but then we remembered that she has six dogs and some students don't like house pets. So we decided to take them to the zoo instead.

Ben: I (not want) 5. _____ to make alternative plans this year. Let's learn about Thai customs on the Internet first.

2 Complete the information they found on the Internet using the expressions below.

You are (not) supposed / expected to . . .   It's (not) considered rude / polite to . . .
You should (always / never). . .   It's (not) okay / acceptable / customary to . . .

In Thailand ....

1. _It is considered rude to_ _____ touch someone on the head.
2. _____take your shoes off when entering a house.
3. _____show your emotions.
4. _____put books on the floor.
5. _____touch a monk.
6. _____show respect to older people.

3 Match the participle modifiers and then complete the sentences.

1. warm	a. haired
2. hard	b. tempered
3. dark	c. working
4. even	d. minded
5. open	e. hearted

1. Thais like to work. They are very _____ people.
2. Many Thais have dark skin and most are _____.
3. It is bad manners in Thailand to lose your temper. Most Thais are very _____.
4. Thais are loving, kind and _____.
5. The Thai people accept other cultures and religions. They are very _____.

4 One of the Thai students is showing Anna some photos. Read their conversation and fill in the blanks with *who* or *which*.

Deng: Would you like to see some photos of Thailand?

Anna: Oh, yes. That would be great.

Deng: This is the town in (1) _____ I live.

Anna: Wow! It's very pretty.

Deng: And this is my family. The person (2) _____ is sitting at the front is my father. And this is the restaurant (3) _____ my father owns.

Anna: Cool! The food looks great. And who's this?

Deng: That's a monk (4) _____ comes to the restaurant every day. We always give him some rice and fish. And this is the school (5) _____ I go to.

Anna: And who is this? Is it your boyfriend? He's cute!

Deng: No, I'm not allowed to have boyfriends right now. It's just the boy (6) _____ sits next to me in class.

5 Use the information in the chart to write an article for the Highbury School magazine.

Event	Comments
Met Thai students at the airport.	Tired and cold.
Took students to a mall to buy warmer clothes.	Some don't speak English very well.
Took students to school.	Took off shoes outside the classroom.
Took students to school dance.	Thais taught us Thai dancing. Great fun.
Invited students to swimming pool.	Canceled trip. None of the students wanted to swim.
Took students for pizza.	Had never eaten cheese before. Some didn't like it.

_____

_____

_____

_____

_____

6 Answer the questions.

1. Why do you think Highbury School invites a group of foreign student every year?

_____

_____

2. How are Thai customs different from your country?

_____

_____

3. What experiences did the Thai students have?

_____

_____

4. Would you like to go to Thailand? Why?

_____

_____

My reading journal 2

1 Look at your prediction for how the story would continue on page 38. How was your prediction different from the real story?

_____

_____

_____

_____

2 In what order did the following events happen? Number the sentences.

____ Oliver and Sylvia jumped out of the window.

____ Mrs. Drummond admitted she was trying to kill Oliver's father..

____ Oliver and Sylvia went in to The Drummond's house.

____ Sylvia read Mrs. Drummond's e-mails.

____ Mrs. Drummond tried to kill Sylvia and Oliver.

____ Alice Drummond returned to the house.

____ Mr. Norman thanked the teens for their great work.

3 Answer the questions.

1. Do you think Oliver and Sylvia should have gone in to Mrs. Drummond's house? Why?

_____

2. Why was Sylvia surprised to discover Mrs. Drummond was the lady in the red dress at Aunt Bertha's birthday party? _____

3. Why did Mrs. Drummond want to kill Oliver's father?

_____

4. How do you think Mrs. Drummond got black oil on her hands?

_____

5. Why is the story called "California Dream"?

_____

4 Match the phrases in each column to describe the characters in the story.

1. Sylvia	a. had a small private plane,	I. and didn't go in to the plane with the others.
2. Oliver	b. is a very determined and intelligent teen,	II. and wanted to kill him so that she could start up in business with a man called Ray.
3. Mrs. Drummond	c. is Mr. Norman's buddy,	III. and was almost killed in the plane crash and by Mrs. Drummond's car.
4. Mr. Norman	d. is Mr. Norman's business partner,	IV. and was almost killed when his car caught fire.
5. Mr. Drummond	e. is Silvia's boyfriend,	V. who discovered who was trying to kill Mr. Norman.

Self check 2

1 **Now I can write sentences using these words.**

1. worried / cheer up _____
2. fix up / beautiful _____
3. hand out / nervous _____
4. interested / interesting _____
5. look for / frightened _____
6. dark-haired / beautiful _____
7. run out of / frustrating _____
8. hard working / satisfaction _____
9. hygienic / safe _____
10. warm-hearted / determined _____

2 **Now I can write sentences using . . .**

1. the hypothetical past (If I had . . . , I would have . . . .)

_____

2. future in the past (I was going to . . .)

_____

3. relative clauses (who, which, that, whose)

_____

4. the passive (. . . was discovered by . . . .)

_____

3 **Now I can . . .**

1. ask polite questions

_____

2. talk about customs in different countries

_____

3. talk about improving the environment

_____

4. talk about doing voluntary work

_____

5. talk about inventions and discoveries

_____